LEAD GUITAR SECRETS

BY KIRK TATNALL

ISBN 978-1-61780-358-1

HAL•LEONARD®
CORPORATION

7777 W. BLUEMOUND RD. P.O. BOX 13819 MILWAUKEE, WI 53213

In Australia Contact:
Hal Leonard Australia Pty. Ltd.
4 Lentara Court
Cheltenham, Victoria, 3192 Australia
Email: ausadmin@halleonard.com.au

Visit Hal Leonard Online at
www.halleonard.com

CD TRACK LISTING

DEMONSTRATION TRACKS

BACKING TRACKS

INTRODUCTION

Welcome to *Lead Guitar Secrets*, a beginner's guide to unlocking the mystery of how to create great guitar solos.

Learning to improvise guitar solos is much like learning to speak a language. In the absolute beginning, a child hears a word and develops an association with it. Upon learning to enunciate it, the child places the word within a context of his or her own, eventually connecting it with other words to express thoughts. At first, words are simple and sentences are short. With time and constant usage, vocabulary increases along with the ability to connect phrases and express longer thoughts. Single words become sentences. Sentences become paragraphs. Paragraphs become chapters. And chapters become complete stories.

Playing guitar solos is no different, and this book will take the same approach to building solos from the ground up. While many books simply give examples of scales and licks, this book focuses on developing your ears and intuition to guide your fingers to the "right" notes, while simultaneously building a rhythmic vocabulary. Together, these two approaches offer the novice improviser a clear path to communicating musically as well as they communicate verbally.

Lead Guitar Secrets is intended for guitarists with some playing experience who wish to branch out and learn to play solos. To eliminate any guesswork as to which position notes should be played in, tablature is used exclusively throughout the book. However, rhythms also are incorporated into the tablature to indicate when to play—and how long to hold—notes. Ideally, guitarists who use this book should know how to count basic rhythms, but the enclosed CD provides audio examples of the musical figures in the book to provide further assistance with learning the material. In a nutshell, *Lead Guitar Secrets* will transform a guitarist who has never improvised into a player who can create guitar solos out of thin air.

In addition to scales, which are like the alphabet from which we construct words, *Lead Guitar Secrets* provides three-, four-, and five-note phrases to develop a rhythmic vocabulary with which to "speak."

Using the Audio CD

Tracks 59–80 on the accompanying audio CD are backing tracks that you can use for soloing over—an extremely helpful practice tool. Specific backing tracks are also referenced throughout the book for practicing particular exercises and sample solos.

CHAPTER 1:

UPPER-OCTAVE MAJOR AND PENTATONIC SCALES

One-Octave Major Scale

The first step in creating a guitar solo is to learn and understand scales. A *scale* is a group of notes that are arranged in a certain intervallic pattern. Most popular music is derived from the *major scale*. Observe the distance between the notes (or intervallic pattern), as shown below, as this is what defines a scale's sound.

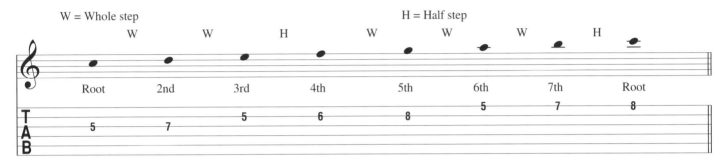

The scale diagrams below illustrate one octave of the major scale. The diagram on the left illustrates the names of the notes, while the diagram on the right illustrates the fingers with which to play them. Memorize this pattern, as we will be moving it around the fretboard to change keys.

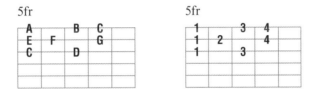

Practice the following exercises while tapping your foot and using alternate picking. Take your time and make sure your pick direction is down on the numbers (1, 2, 3, and 4), and up on the "ands." Accuracy is more important than speed. Feel free to move further into the book while keeping these patterns in your practice routine.

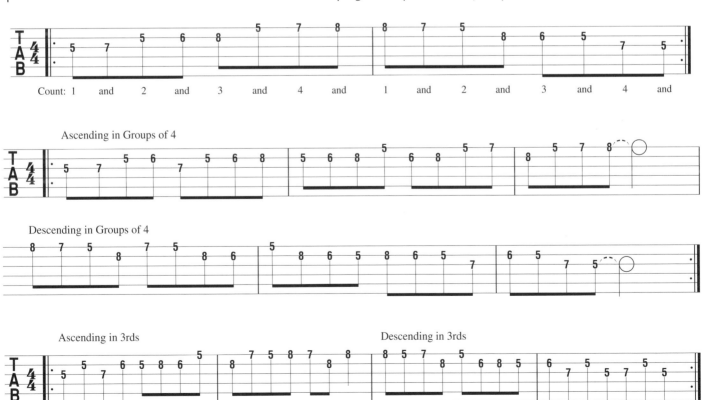

One-Octave Pentatonic Scale

The *pentatonic scale* derives its name from the fact that the scale contains five tones (penta = five). The major pentatonic scale is constructed from the major scale by removing two notes, the 4th and the 7th. The increased distance between the 3rd and the 5th and between the 6th and the root give the scale its unique sound. Study the two scales below, observing the differences in the distances between the notes.

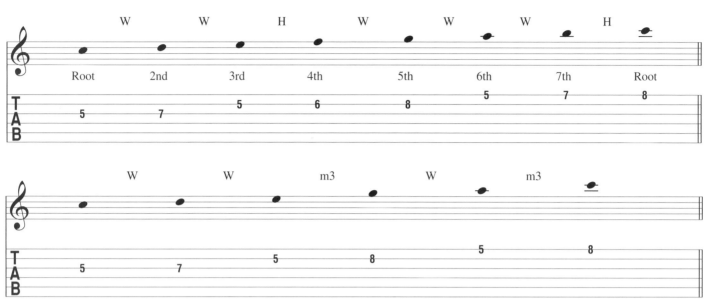

m3 = minor 3rd (three half steps)

Many guitar solos are based upon combining the sounds of the major scale with the pentatonic scale. As with the previous examples, the diagram on the left illustrates the names of the notes, while the diagram on the right illustrates the fingers with which to play them. Commit these diagrams to memory so they can be freely moved to different keys.

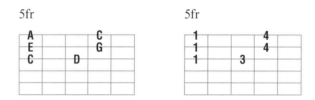

Once again, make sure you tap your foot and use alternate picking while practicing the exercises below. The goal is to train your pick hand to automatically pick in the correct direction so the thought never enters your mind while improvising. The exercises below will become useful melodic patterns that you can improvise with later. Feel free to move further into the book while keeping these patterns in your daily practice routine.

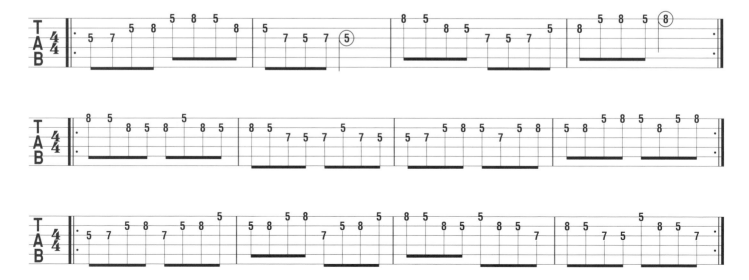

FINDING THE STRONGEST NOTES

Let's take a quick look at where chords come from. You can build a chord from any note of the major scale by picking a starting note and skipping up the scale in 3rds (the distance between the notes). In the example below, we start on the note C and skip every other note, giving us the root, 3rd, and 5th of the scale. Play an open C chord and observe how its notes are all Cs (roots), Es (3rds), and Gs (5ths).

When it comes to making melodies, the scale notes from which the chord is built will resonate strongest, with no tension whatsoever. Pitches from the scale that are not used in the chord itself will "pull" to those pitches that are in the chord. To begin examining this idea, we will start with the pentatonic scale. Since it is a five-note scale and contains three chord tones, only two notes, the 2nd and the 6th, pull to chord tones. The 2nd will either pull down to the root or up to the 3rd, and the 6th will pull down to the 5th or up to the root. Notice how the scale diagram now shows the pattern as degrees of the scale to help you identify where the tensions and releases are located.

Play the following exercise with Backing Track 59 and listen closely to each note, observing how each scale degree sits with the chord. This is the first step in learning Lead Guitar Secret No. 1: Let the notes pull you!

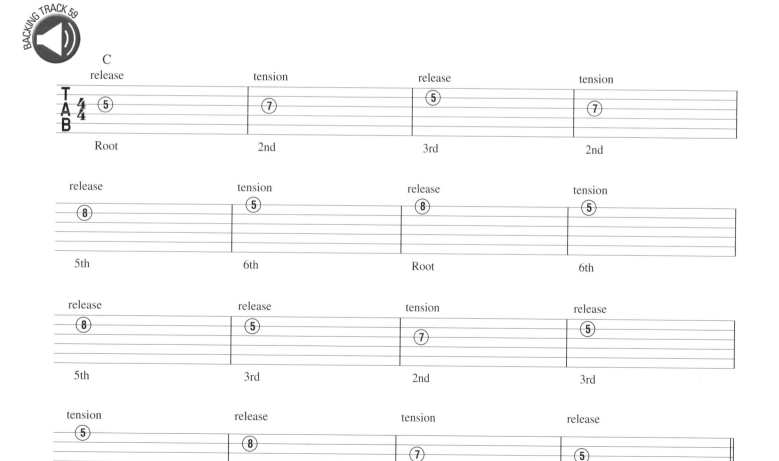

EXAMINING "PULLS" IN THE MAJOR SCALE

Before we begin to explore this concept with the major scale, we need to add the 4th and the 7th to the scale pattern, as shown below.

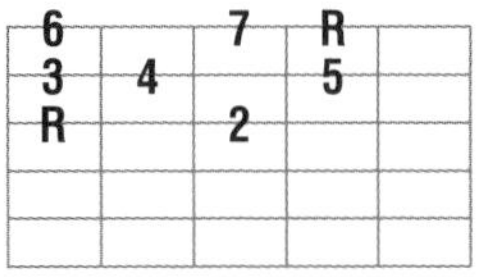

The addition of these pitches introduces some new tensions and resolutions. While these are not absolute rules, resolutions often occur in this manner:

→ The 2nd pulls down to the root or up to the 3rd;

→ The 4th pulls down to the 3rd or up to the 5th;

→ The 6th pulls down to the 5th;

→ The 7th, often referred to as the "leading tone," pulls up to the root;

→ The 6th and the 7th can be played in a three-note phrase that leads up to the root or down to the 5th.

Take your time with the next exercise, focusing on the feeling of resolution as the notes pull you towards chord tones. Again, play this along with Backing Track 59 so you can hear the notes against a C chord.

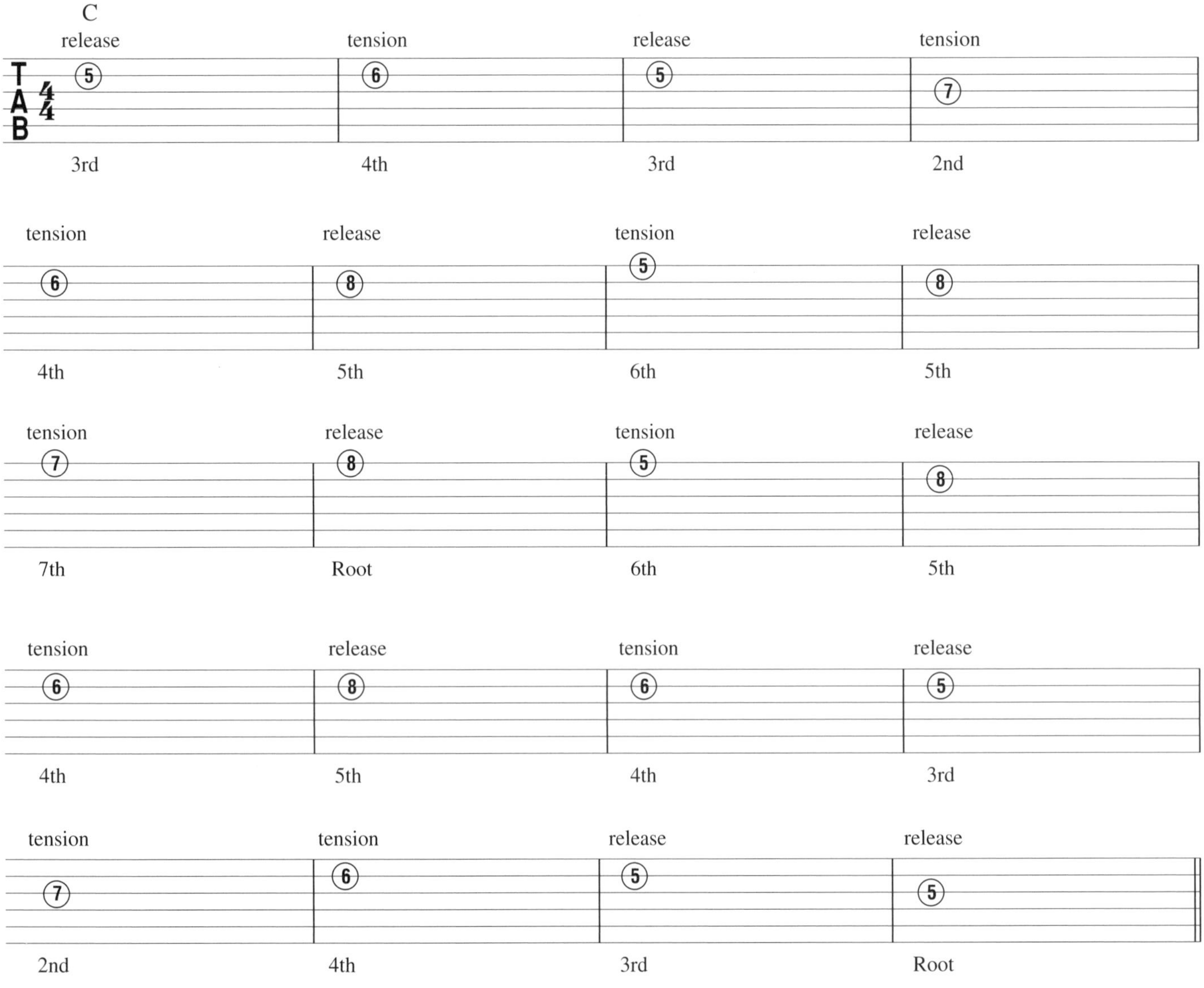

VIBRATO

While we are taking the time to play slowly and to hear how different scale tones feel when played over a chord, it is a good opportunity to introduce *vibrato*. By definition, vibrato is a pulsating effect that is produced by slight and rapid variations in pitch. Vibrato is used to add expression and vocal-like qualities to instrumental music.

Using vibrato enables you to sound like a pro, turning the simplest of melodies into powerful statements. However, vibrato also can be quite a challenge to master, as the number of ways to apply vibrato rivals the number of guitar players that inhabit the planet. Let's examine the two most popular types of vibrato, vertical and horizontal.

The most common type, vertical vibrato is created by slightly bending the string either up or down, perpendicular to the length of the string. To ensure that they stay on the neck, string 1 must be pushed up and string 6 must be pushed down. The remaining strings, however, can be bent in either direction, depending on your preference at that particular moment.

Slightly less common, yet still highly effective, horizontal vibrato produces a more subtle effect by pushing and pulling the note with a motion that runs parallel to the string. When executed correctly, pushing the string towards the bridge will make the note sound slightly flat and pulling it towards the nut will make it sound slightly sharp. Horizontal vibrato is accomplished without any perpendicular bending whatsoever. Lighter string gauges and nylon-string guitars better facilitate this technique.

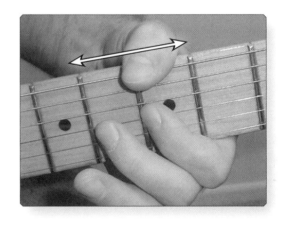

Vibrato Tips:

➡ Relax and go slowly;

➡ Always make sure that the note returns to its original pitch. The mark of a beginner is vibrato that quivers too fast and makes the note sound out of tune;

➡ Before initiating the vibrato, let the original pitch sound clearly. If you start the vibrato before the original pitch sounds, the note will sound sharp.

Listen to the following audio example and use the "good vibrato" as a benchmark for your own vibrato technique. For further practice, play the previous two exercises while applying vibrato.

RHYTHM AND PHRASING

Until this point, we mainly have been discussing which notes to play. The other side of the musical coin is *when* and *where* we place the notes, more commonly known as *rhythm* and *phrasing*. Rhythm gives a melody motion and is just as important as what notes are played.

The following solos are designed to help you develop a rhythmic vocabulary from which you can draw, while simultaneously developing the concept of letting the melodies steer you towards the notes that sit best with the chord you are playing over.

First, get a feel for the basic rhythm of each solo example with the provided "Rhythm" line. Then listen to and play along with the recording of the first line of the solo. When you are comfortable with it, learn the remainder of the solo without the recording. Then, when you are ready, play the solo with Backing Track 59. Lastly, continue improvising with the stated rhythm, experimenting with your note choices and paying close attention to how they resonate with the chord that you are soloing over.

C Major Solo 1

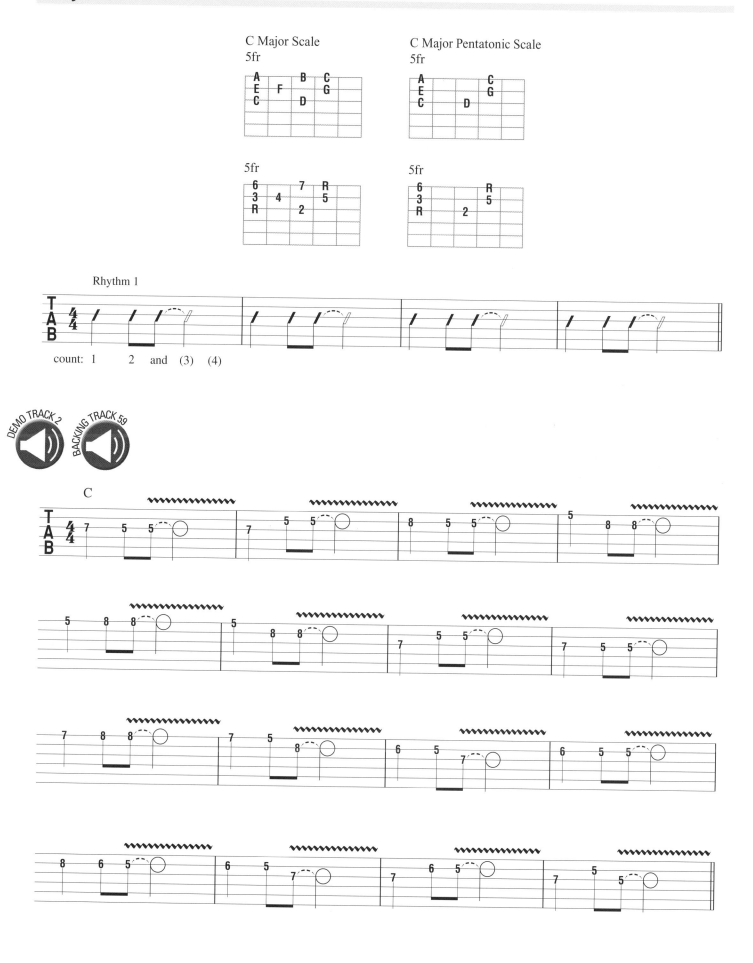

C Major Solo 2

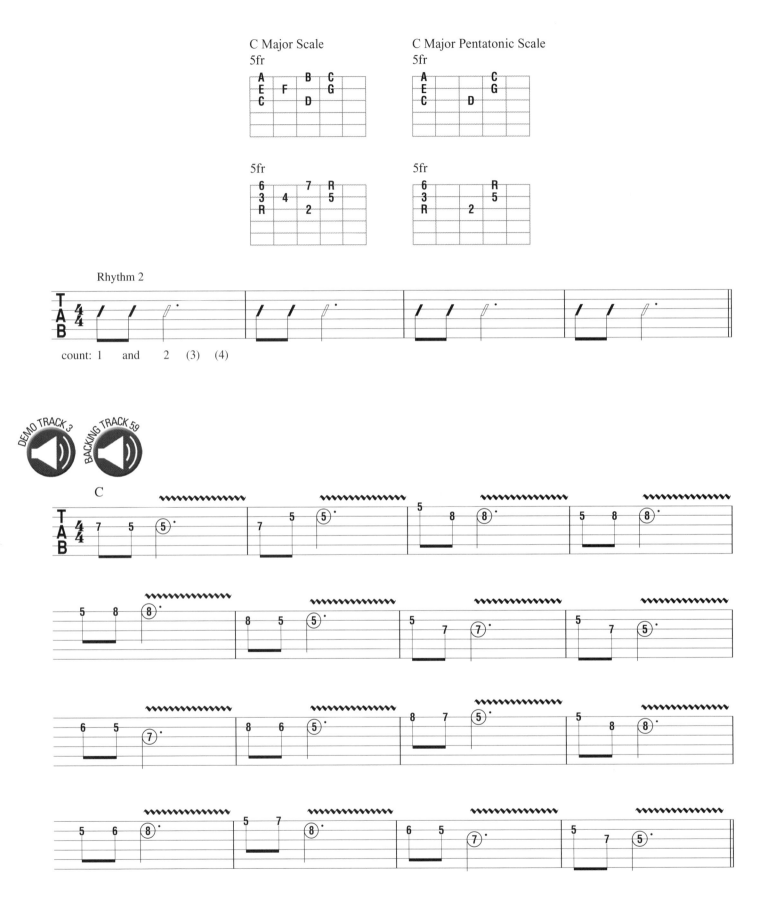

MOVING THE SCALE PATTERN

As we move into different keys, we simply need to move our scale fingerings to different locations on the fretboard. At first, changing keys can be challenging, considering that the frets are spaced differently and the fretboard dots are in different locations. Fortunately, the fingering remains consistent. Practice the following melodic patterns, in the key of A major, while getting used to the new spacing.

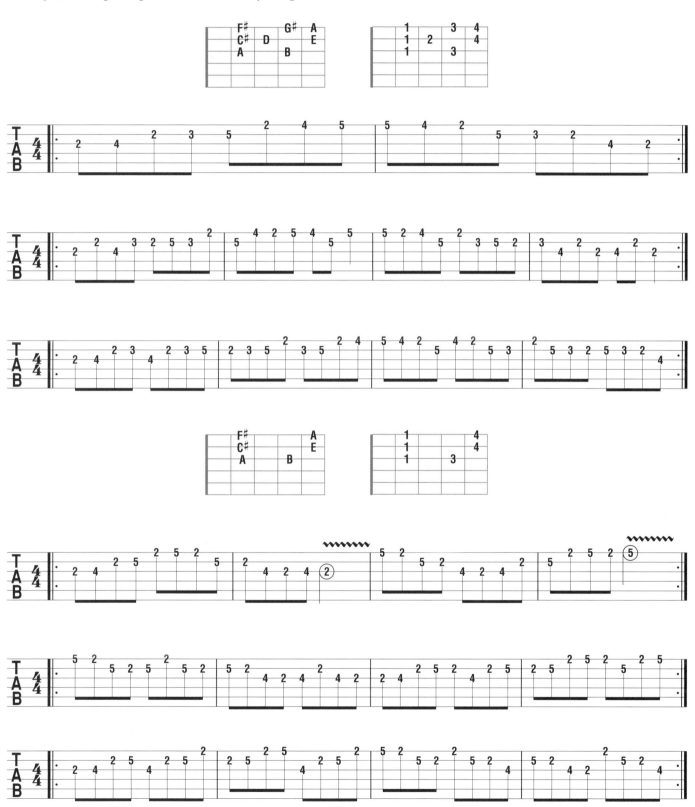

Follow the same process as earlier with the following solo exercises.

A Major Solo

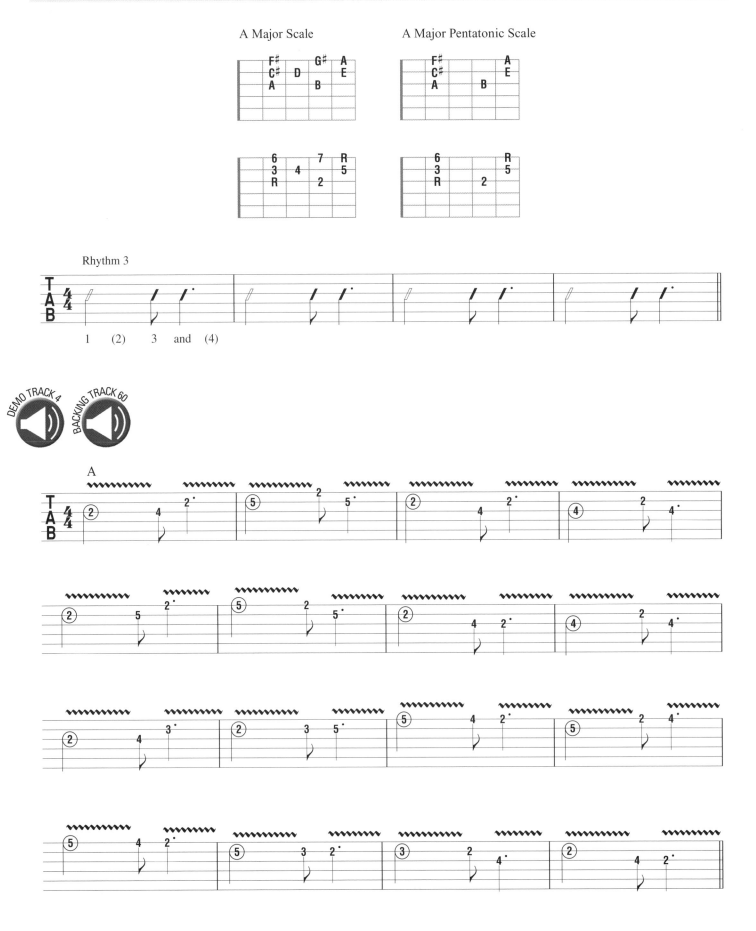

A Major Scale

A Major Pentatonic Scale

Rhythm 3

1   (2)   3   and   (4)

G Major Solo 1 (12th Position)

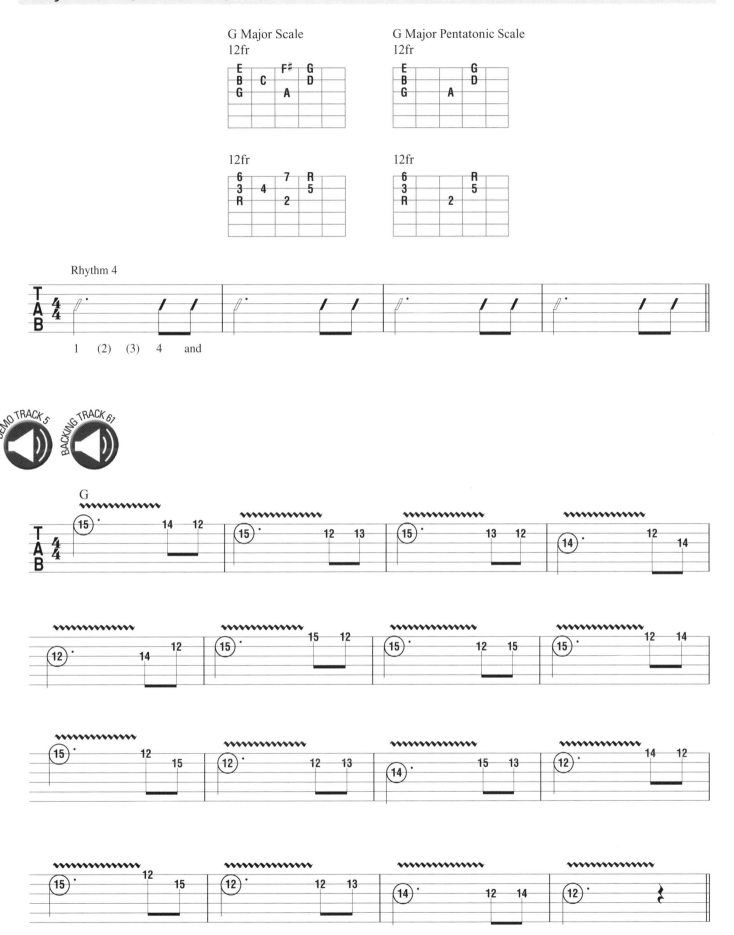

G Major Solo 2 (Open Position)

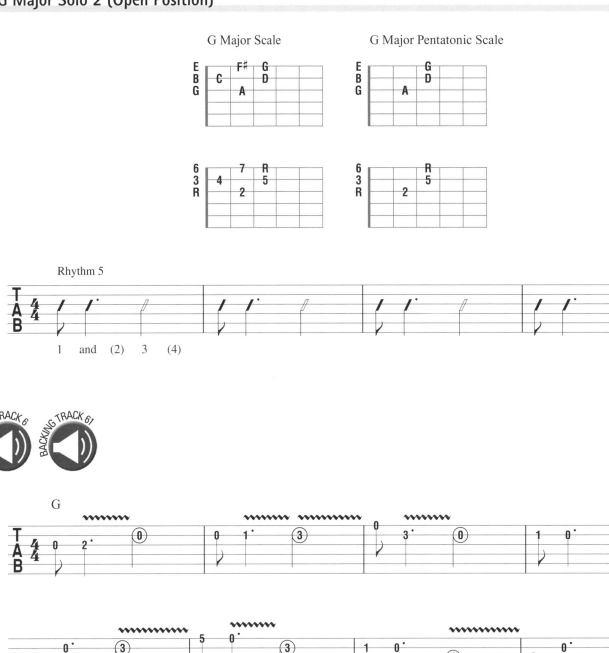

G Major Scale

G Major Pentatonic Scale

Rhythm 5

1 and (2) 3 (4)

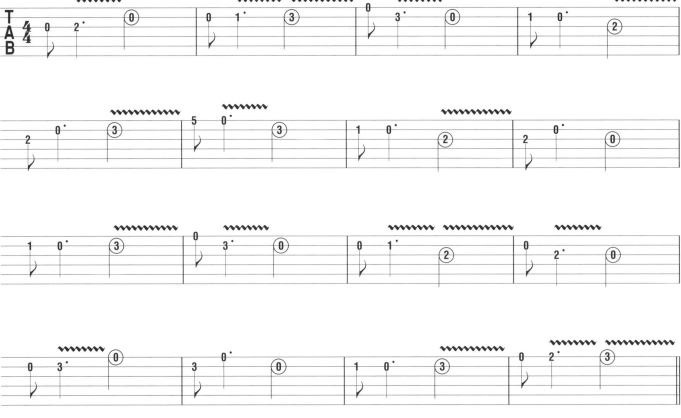

G

CHAPTER 2:

LOWER-OCTAVE MAJOR AND PENTATONIC SCALES

Exploring the Lower-Octave Major Scale

Now that you have gained some experience with the upper octave of the major scale, it is time to add strings 4–6 to the picture and extend the scale into the next octave. Notice that, in the following exercises, we've included two notes on string 3 to complete the octave.

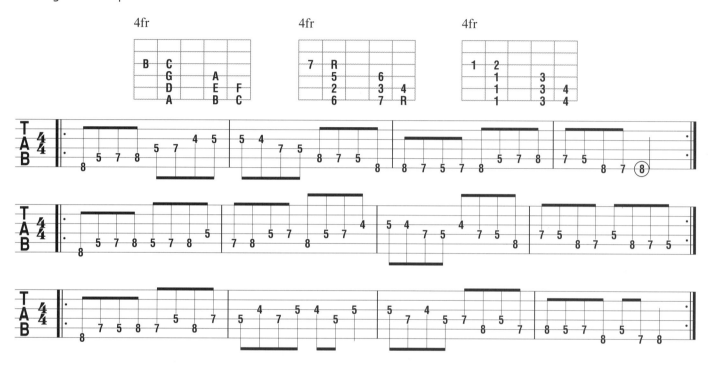

Exploring the Lower-Octave Pentatonic Scale

Like the major scale, here the major pentatonic scale is extended into the lower octave.

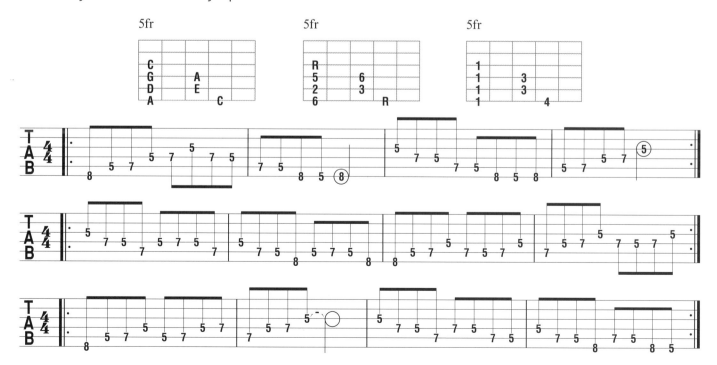

Study and play the following solo exercises as you did with the upper-octave examples in the last chapter.

C Major Solo

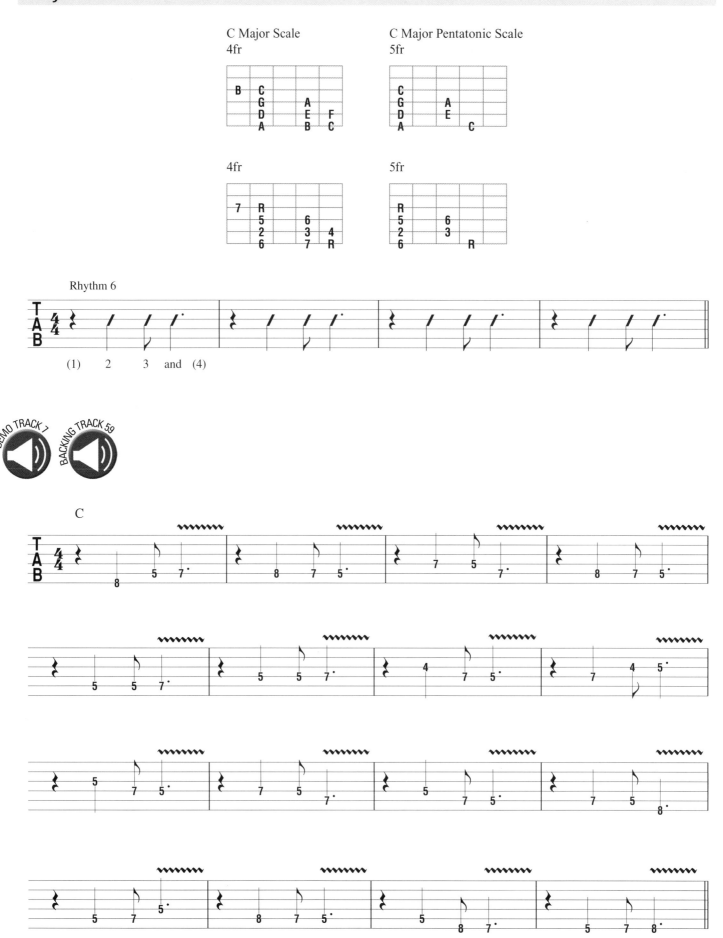

D Major Solo

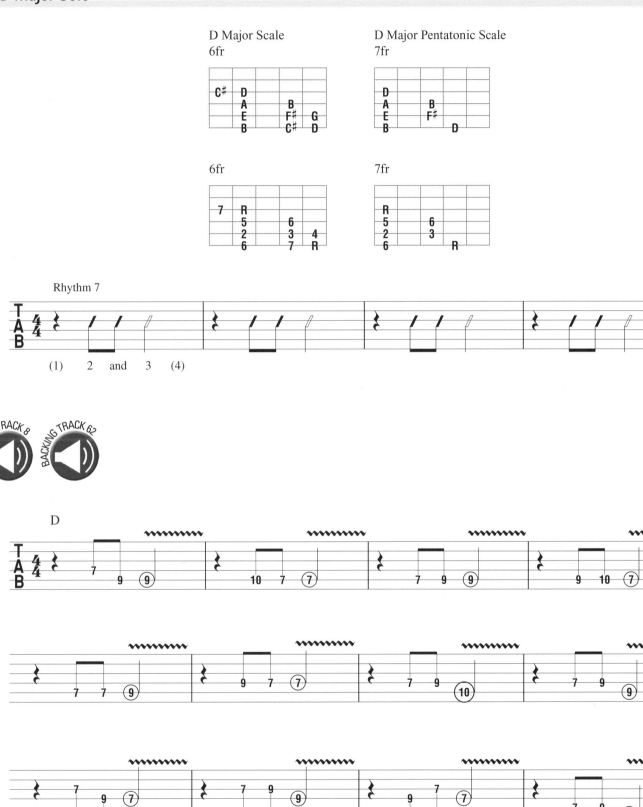

B♭ Major Solo

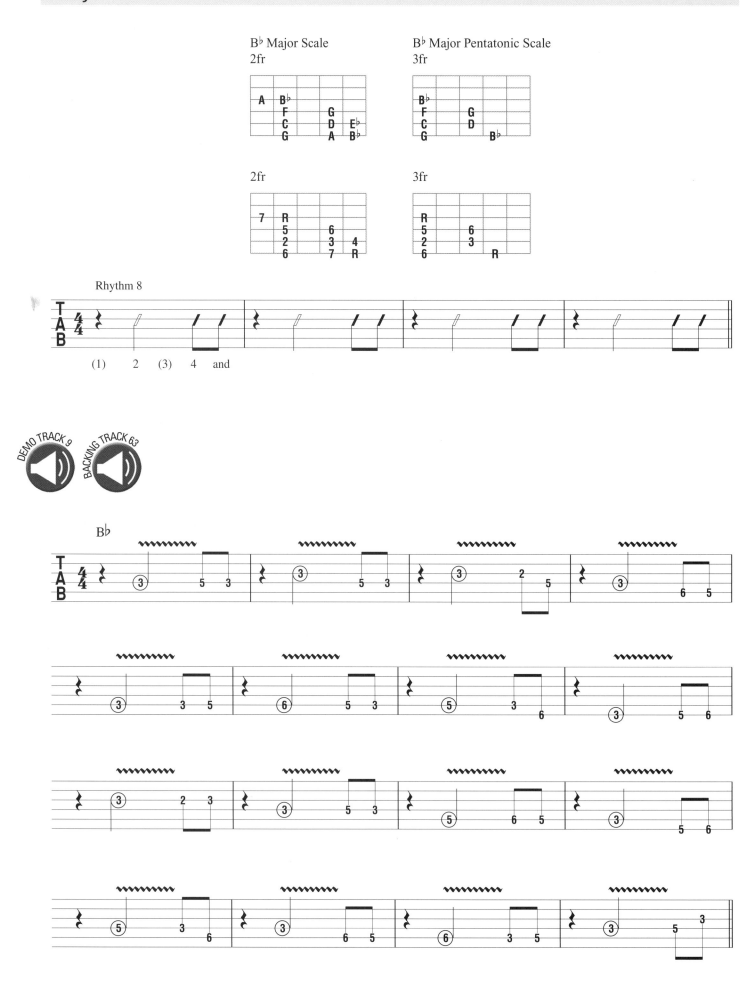

E Major Solo

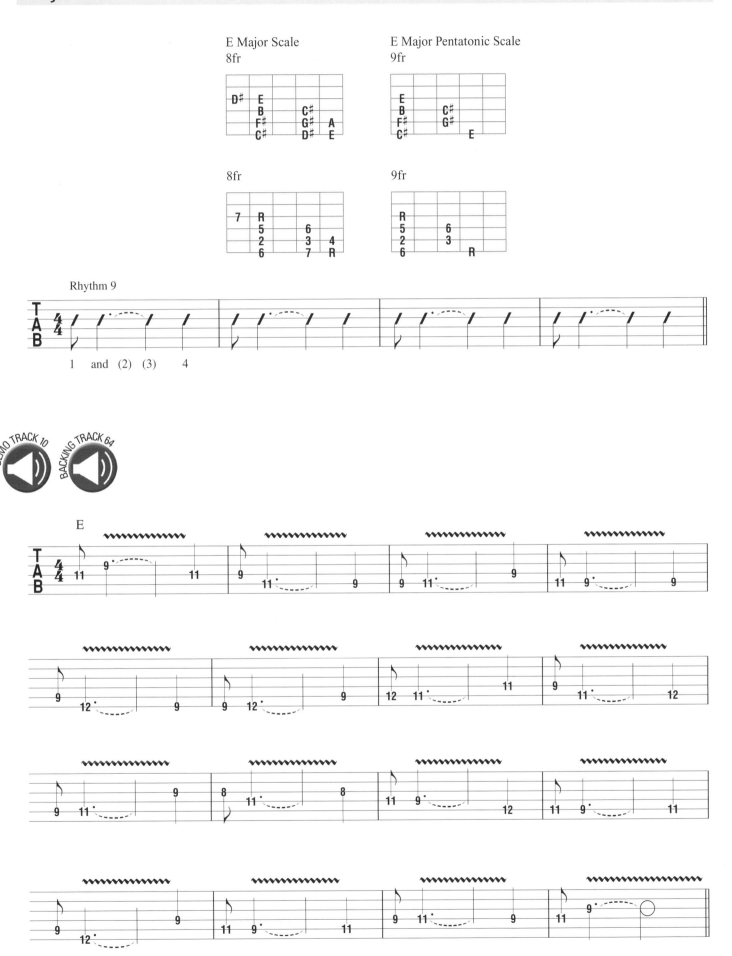

E♭ Major Solo

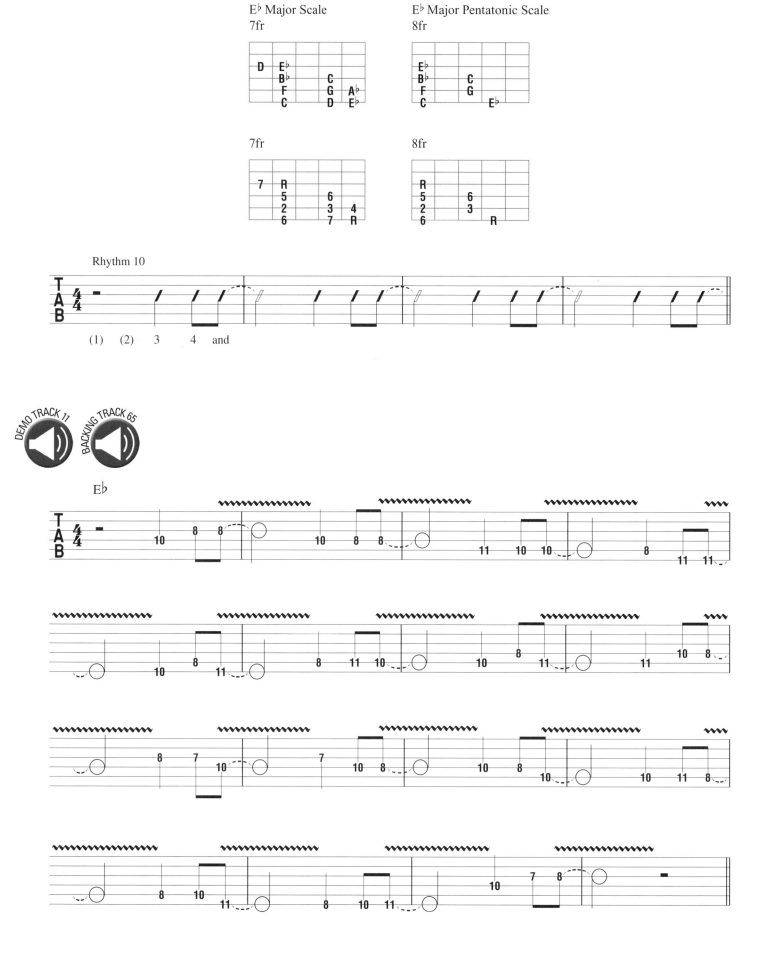

CHAPTER 3:
TWO-OCTAVE MAJOR AND PENTATONIC SCALES

Utilizing the Full Two-Octave Major and Pentatonic Scales

The following diagrams and exercises feature the full two-octave major pentatonic and major scales from the previous chapters.

C Major Pentatonic Scale

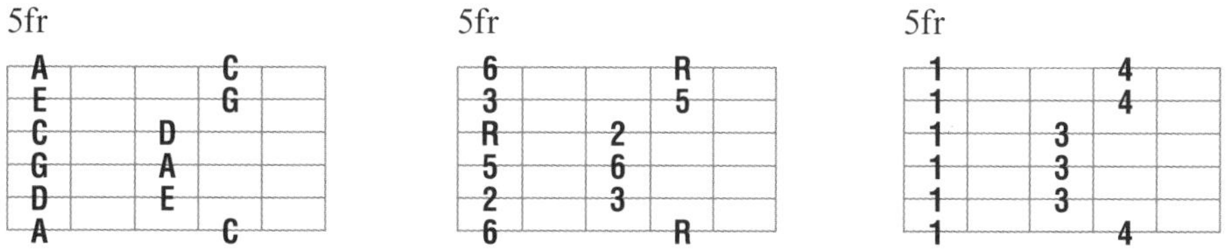

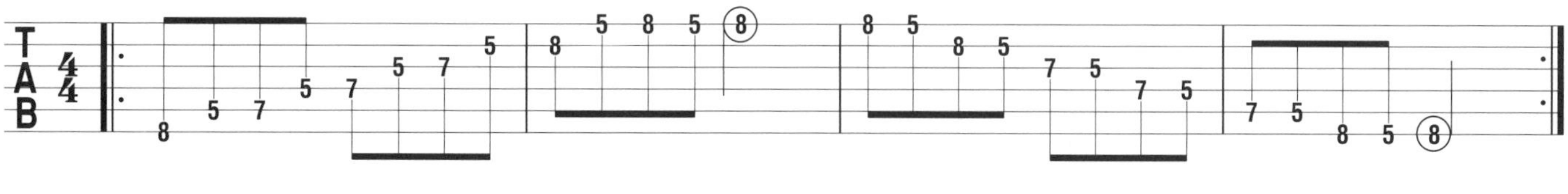

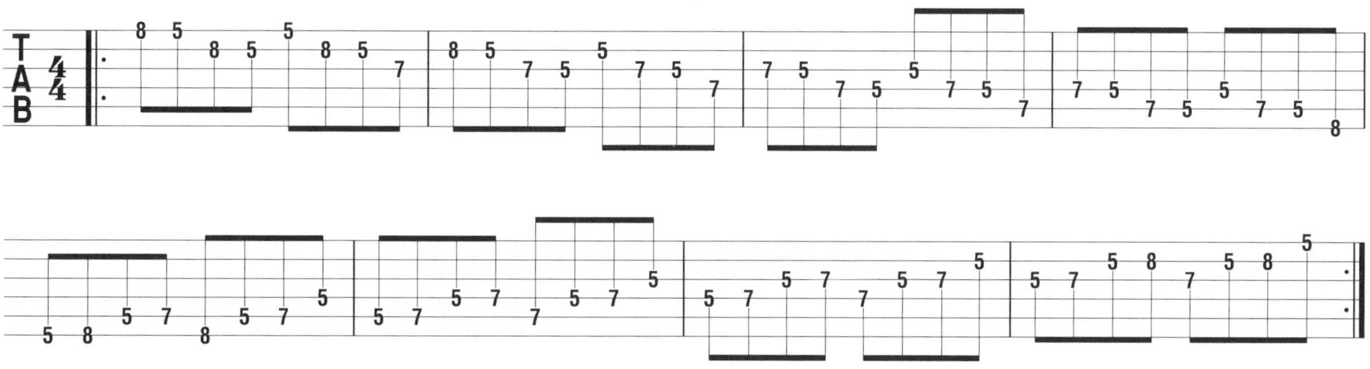

C Major Scale

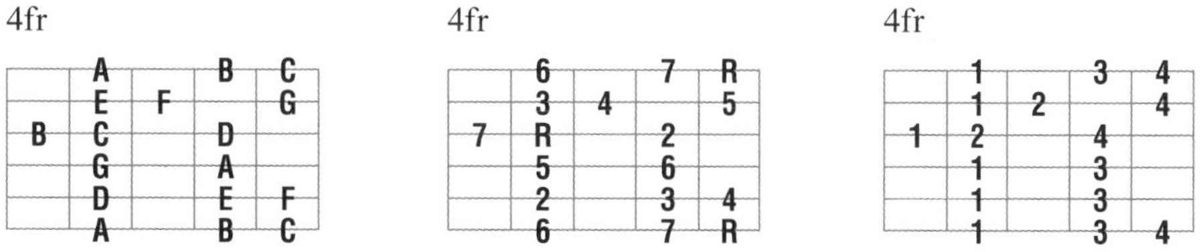

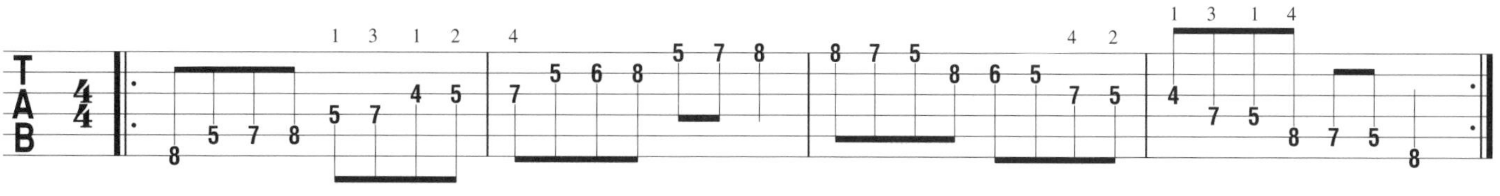

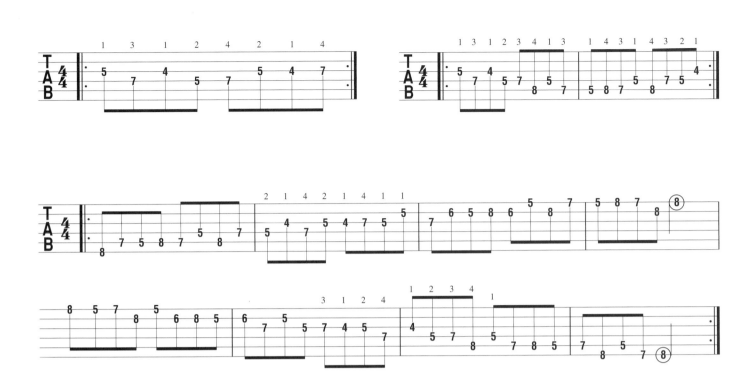

RHYTHM REVIEW

By playing the ten solos found in Chapters 1 and 2, you have added ten rhythmic patterns to your musical vocabulary! Review the patterns by counting them out loud, then go back to any of the previous backing tracks and improvise over them freely, using those rhythms in any way that you choose (i.e., mix and match). The only limit is your imagination!

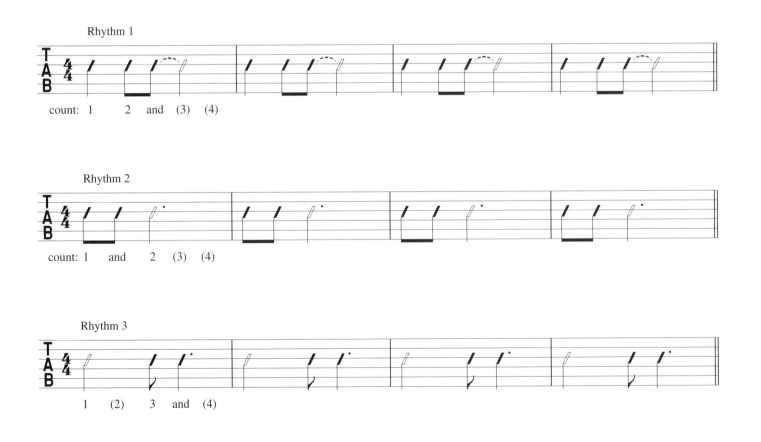

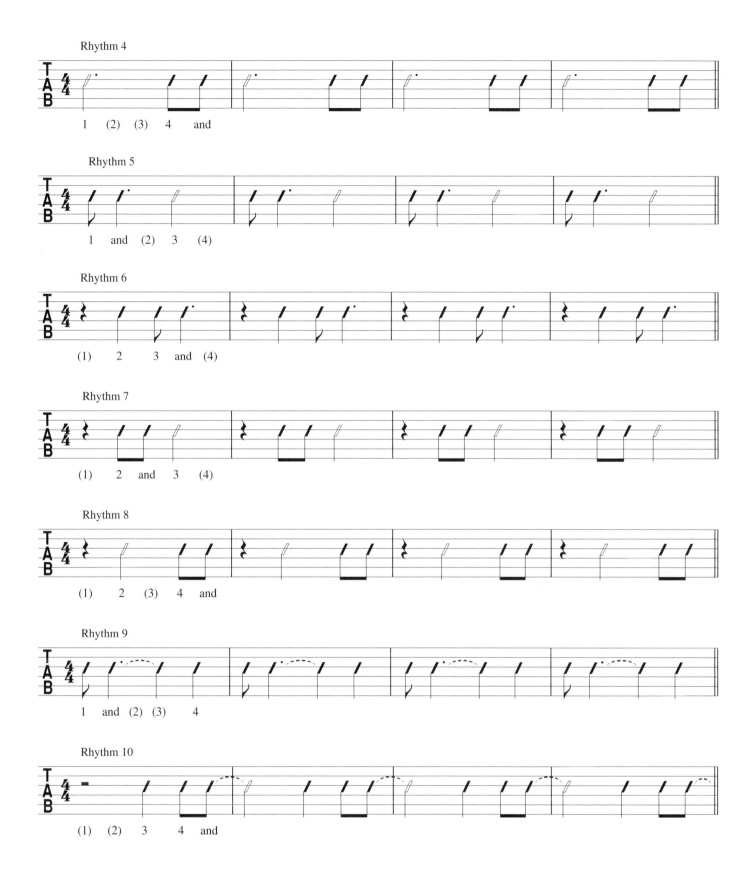

In the following three sample solos, we will combine all of the material that we've learned so far. All of the tools are labeled to illustrate how you might string them together on the spot, in a real improvisation. Take note of how the melodic patterns are interspersed among the rhythms that we've learned to build motion or act as connectors.

C Major Solo

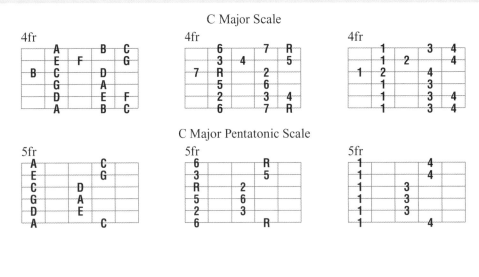

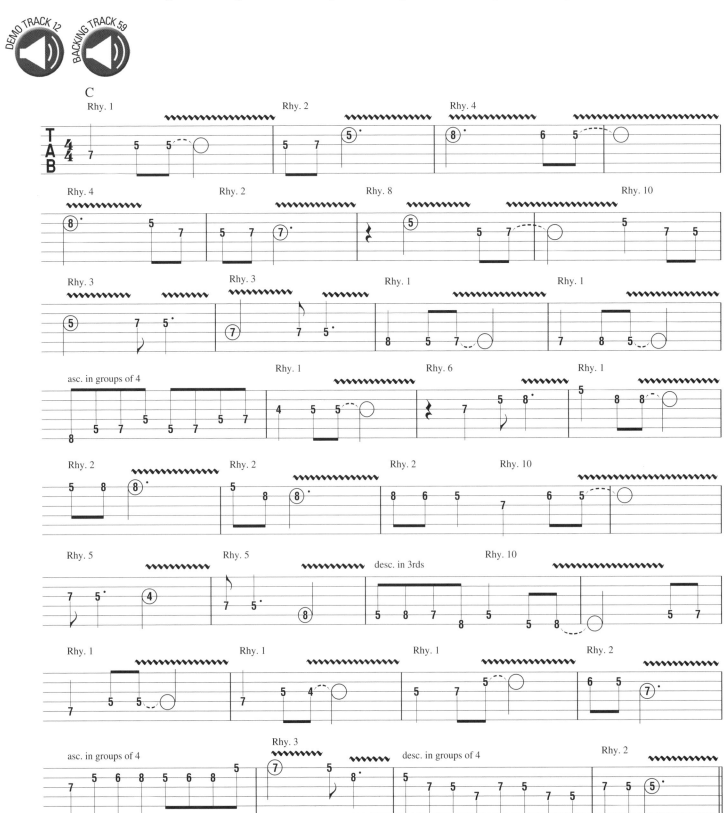

28

E Major Solo

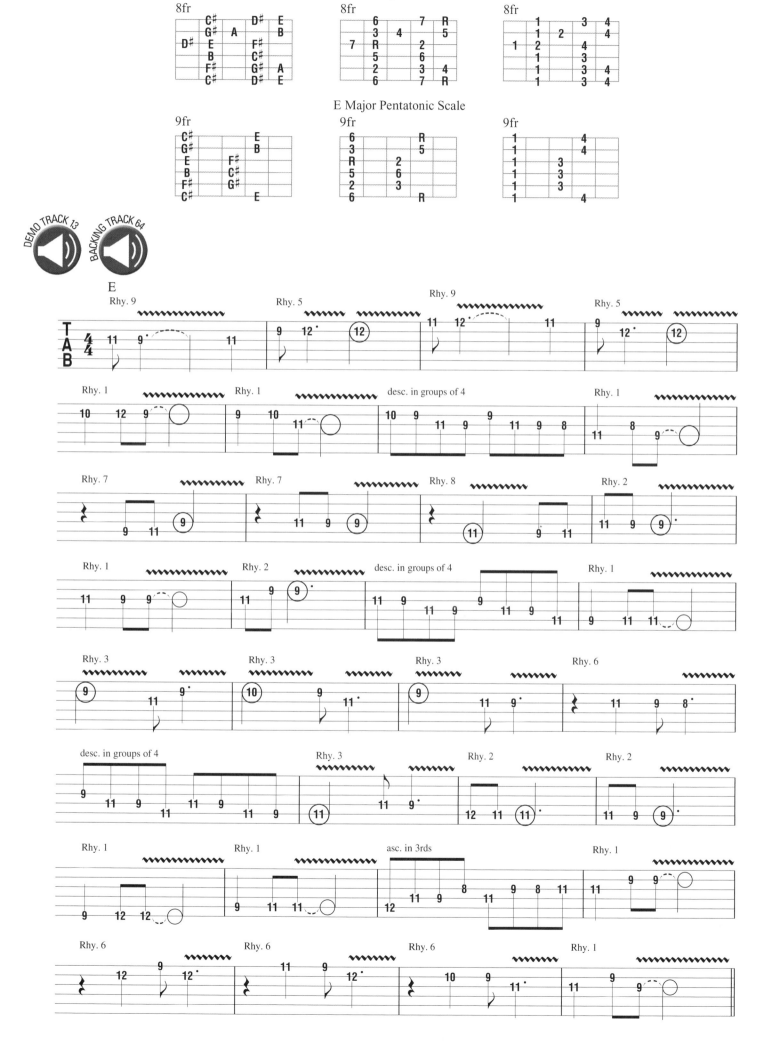

A Major Solo

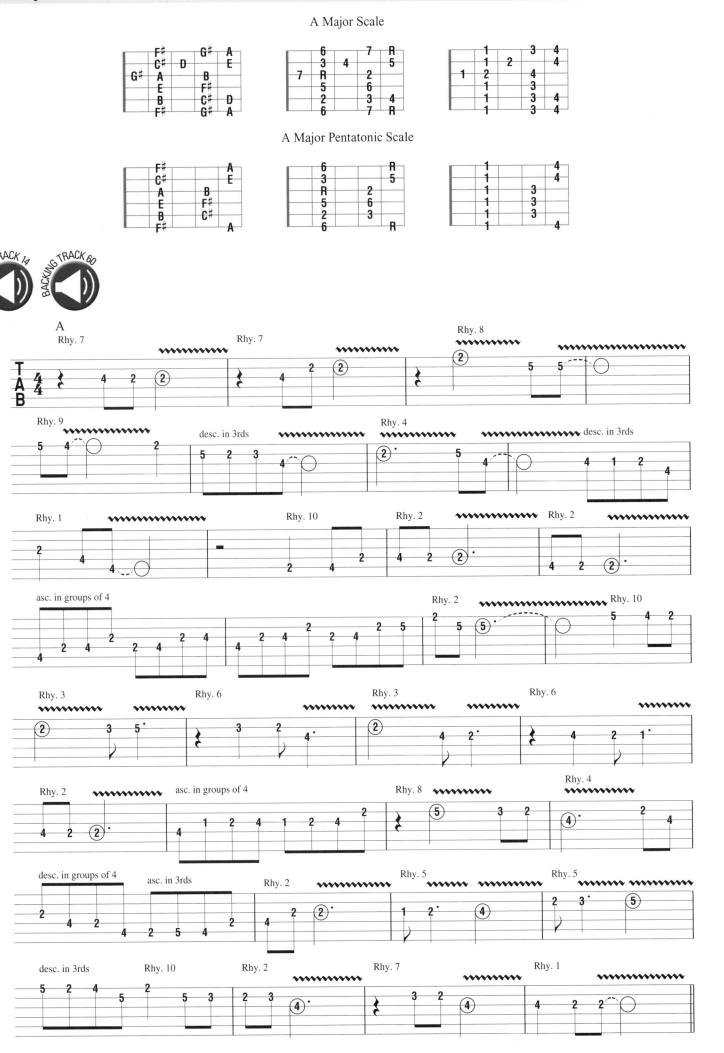

CHAPTER 4:

LEARNING THE SOUND OF VI MINOR

Until this point of the book, we have been dealing solely with the sound of the major chord, or the I chord. As stated earlier in the book, a chord can be built from any note of the major scale by starting on that note and skipping up the scale in 3rds. For review, examine how we accomplished this by using the C major scale.

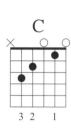

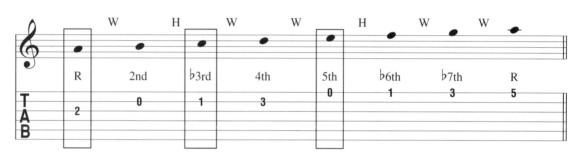

One of the most popular notes from which to build a new chord is the 6th. To do so, we start by using the major scale that we've learned, C major, and start from its sixth step, A, as shown below.

Although this scale is simply a C major scale that is started from A, doing so creates a new interval pattern. The half step that is located between the 2nd and 3rd lowers the 3rd a half step. Typically, an A chord would contain a C♯, but our chord, built from the 6th of C major, contains a C natural. This note is referred to as a lowered 3rd or minor 3rd (♭3rd). This note is the determining factor in whether a chord is major or minor. Also, note how the new intervallic pattern changes the sixth and seventh steps of the scale. Strum the Am chord, then play the scale.

Since this scale was created from the notes of C major, none of the fingerings that we've learned thus far will change. What will change, however, is the way that we look at the notes and which notes become the strongest notes on which to land. In the following scale diagrams, observe how the fretboard locations of the notes have not changed, but the labels of the scale degrees now reflect the new order of the notes. Next, observe where our new target notes (A, C, and E) lie within the scale pattern.

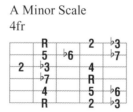

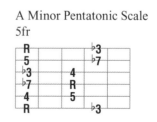

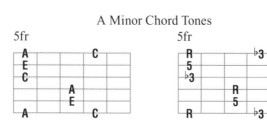

NEW MELODIC PATTERNS

To aid in the absorption of the sound of our new chord, we will introduce some new melodic patterns. When learning a new pattern, examining a small segment of the pattern to hear how it works can be very helpful. This approach will enable you to reuse the pattern at will from different notes of the scale when improvising, as well as to cement it into your musical vocabulary. The following exercises group the pentatonic scale in a pattern of 3s.

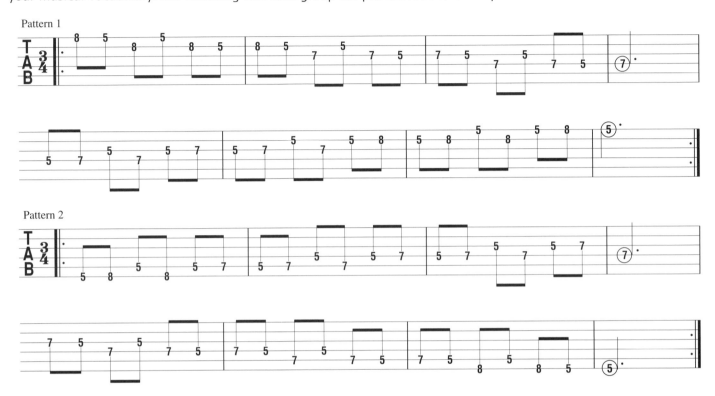

Our next two exercises use the full A minor scale and can be thought of as "three and a 3rd." Each pattern plays three notes of the scale, then skips an interval of a 3rd. Notice that the sound of the scale is determined by where the patterns stop and start.

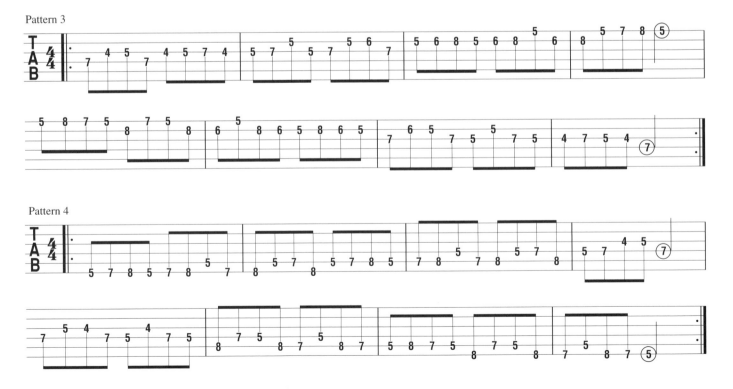

Continue to practice these patterns daily while advancing to the next section.

A Minor Solo

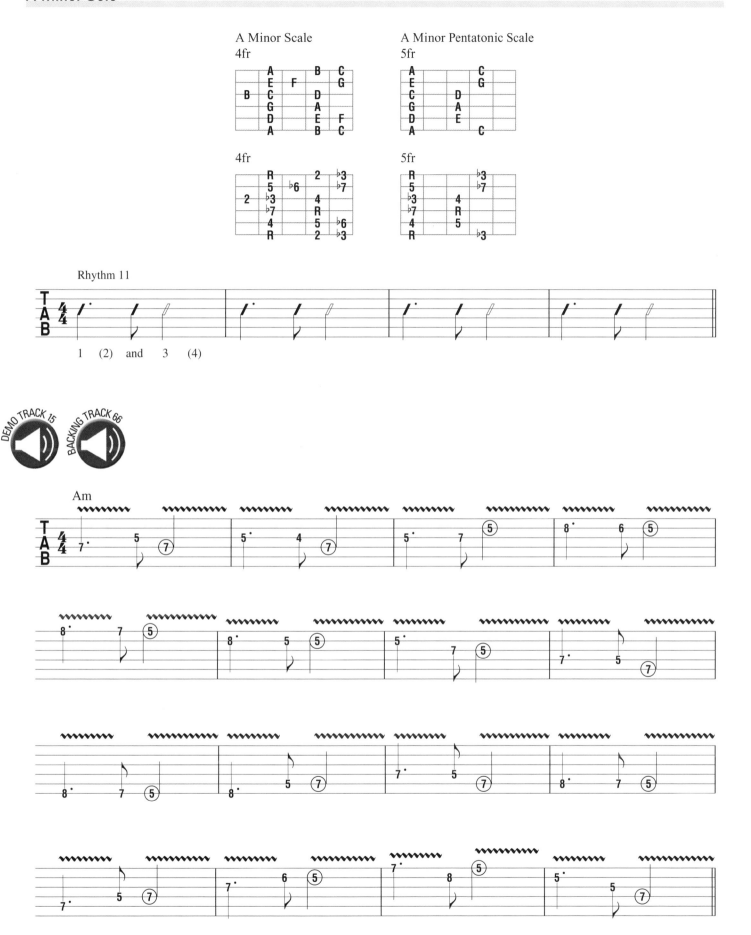

C Minor Solo

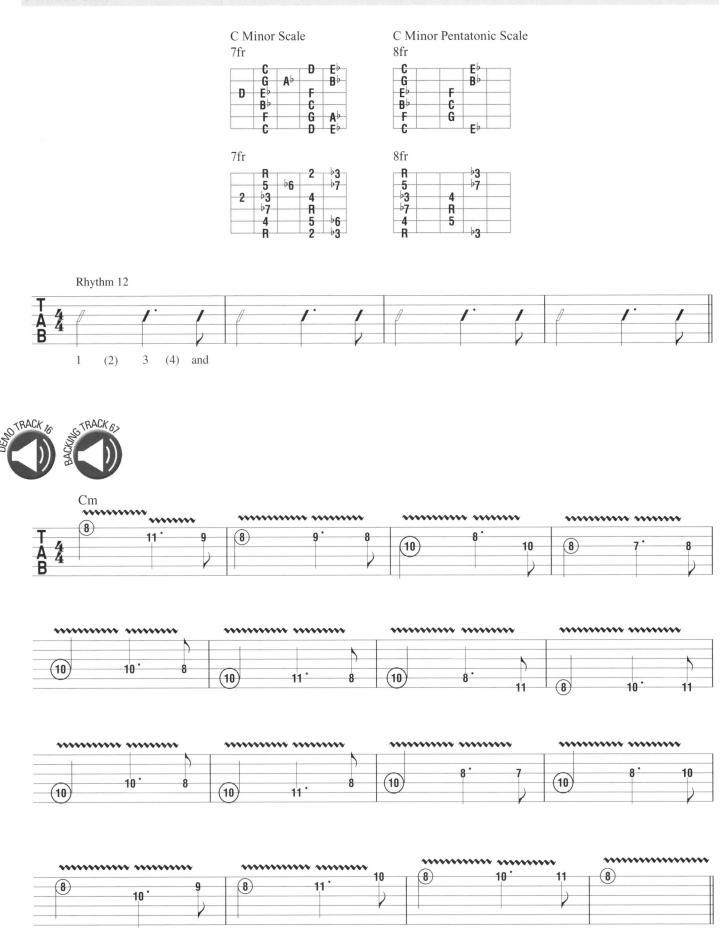

E Minor Solo

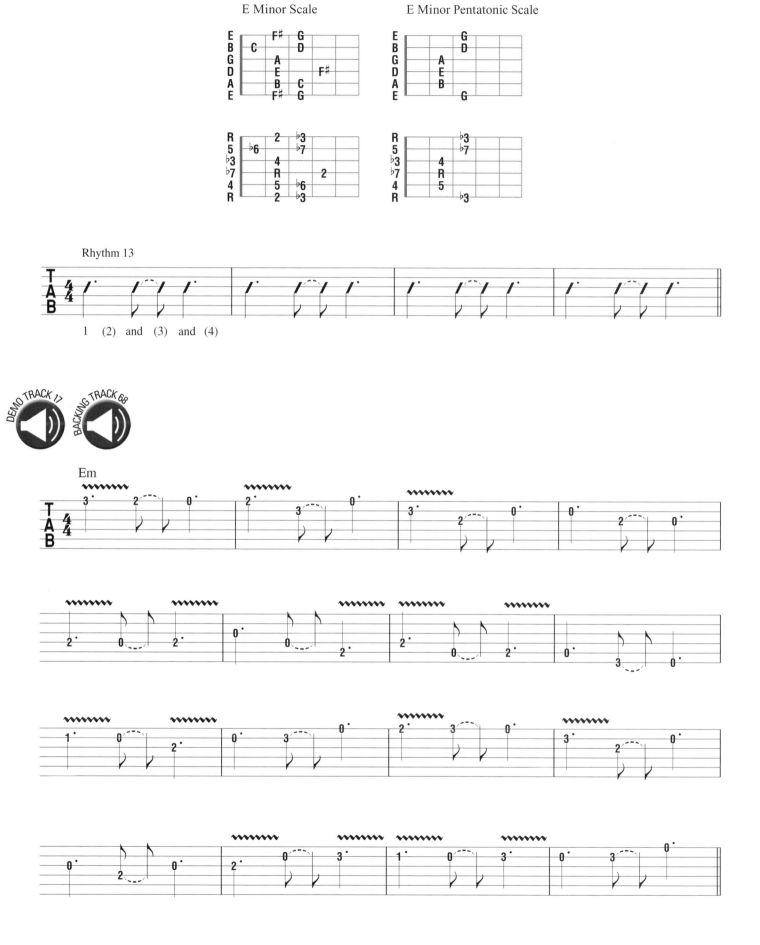

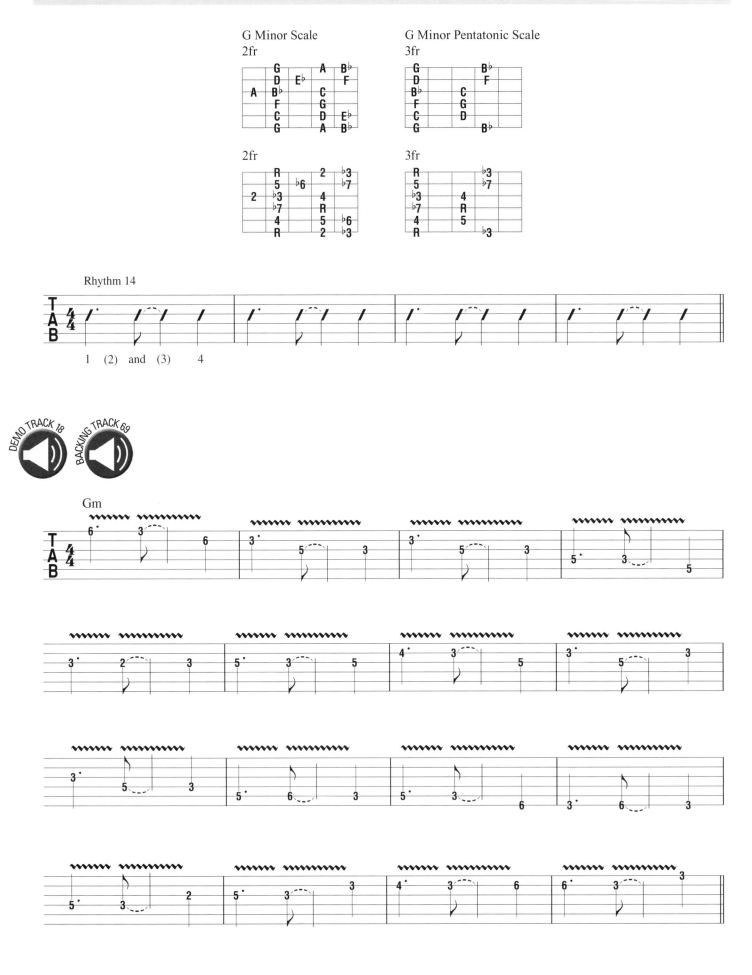

D Minor Solo

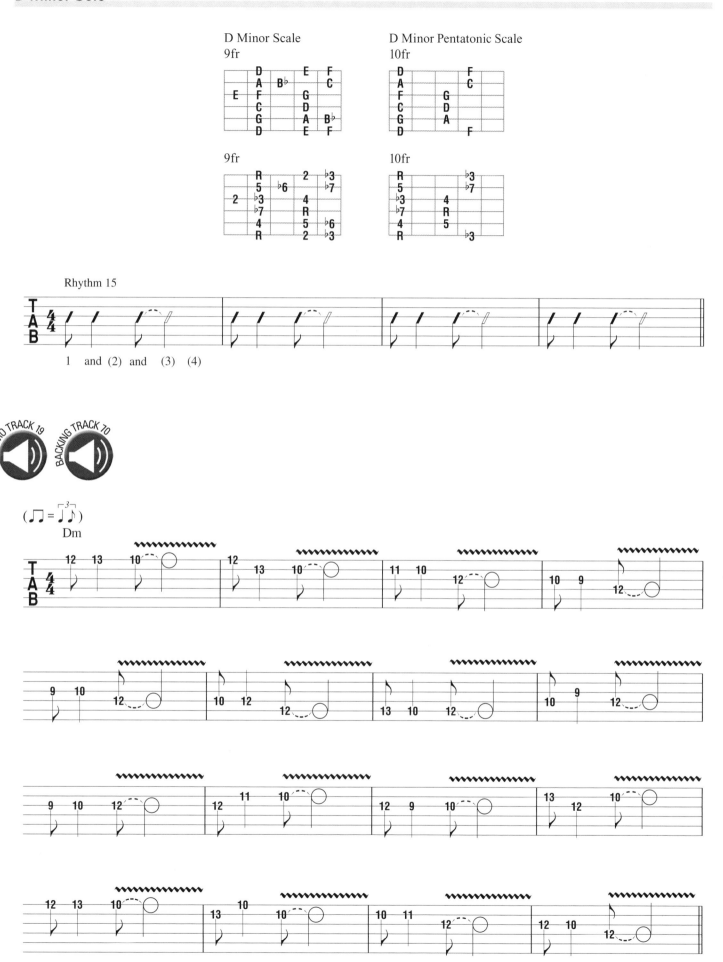

CHAPTER 5:

COMBINING I MAJOR AND VI MINOR

Before we begin to solo over two different chords, it is helpful to examine where the strongest notes of each chord are located by playing some arpeggios. An *arpeggio* is simply the notes of a chord played individually. Play the first portion of the following exercise as it's written, observing how each note sounds over the chord, then continue to improvise over Backing Track 71, using only chord tones. Doing so will focus entirely on the sound of each chord.

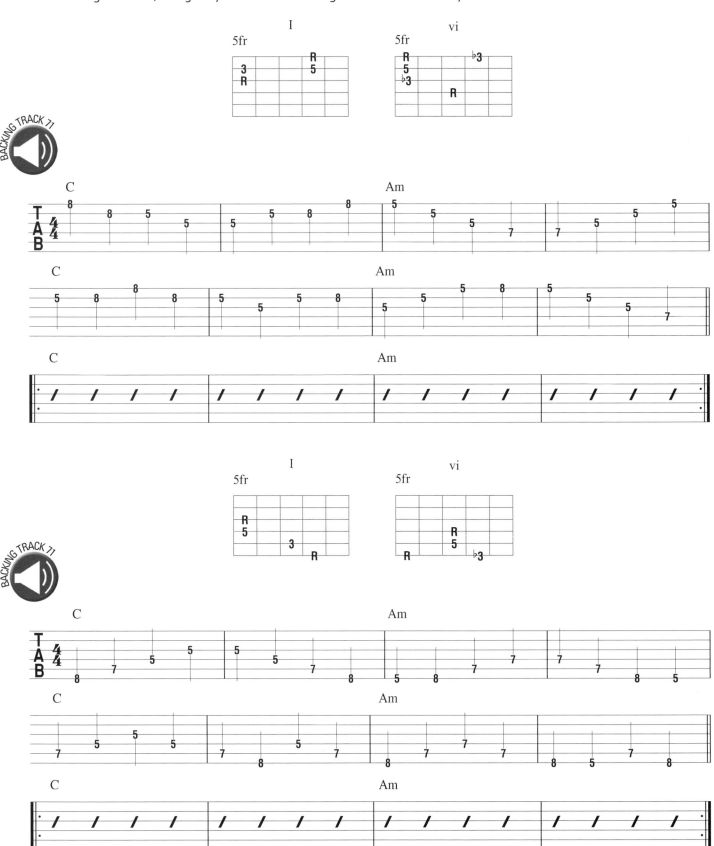

In the following example solos, continue to be aware of how the lines resolve to notes that are consonant with the chord. Before playing the solo, use the arpeggio diagrams to review the major and minor arpeggios.

C–to–Am Solo

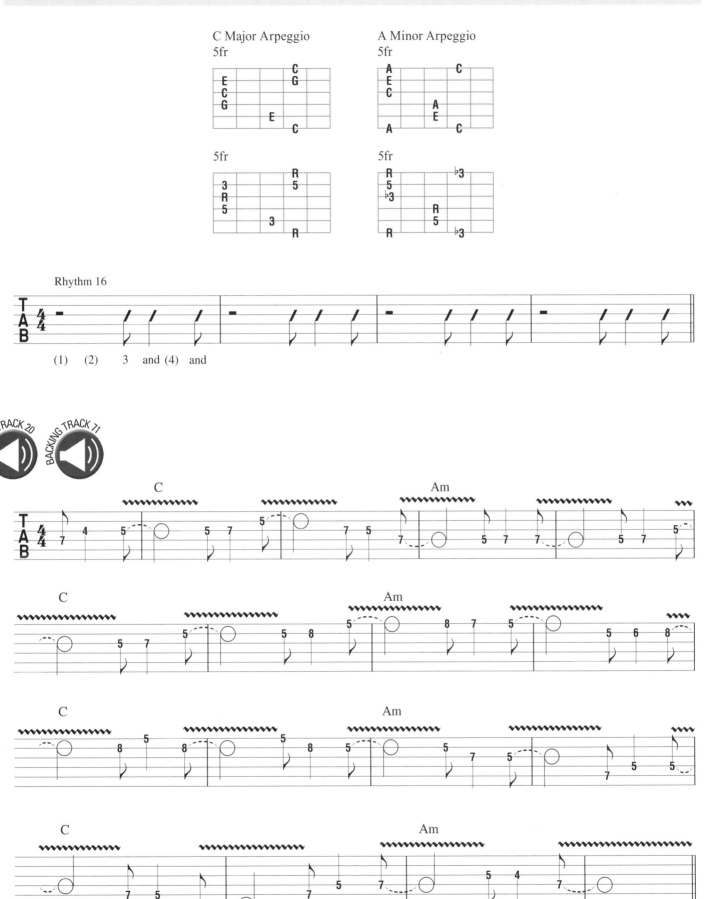

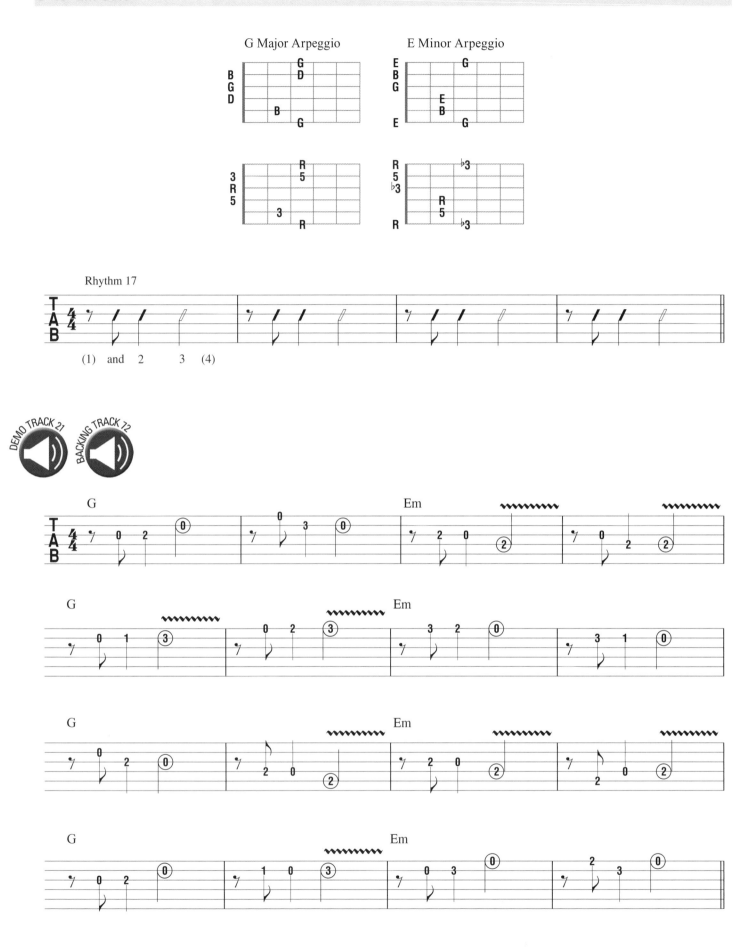

G Major Arpeggio

E Minor Arpeggio

A-to-F#m Solo

A Major Arpeggio   F# Minor Arpeggio

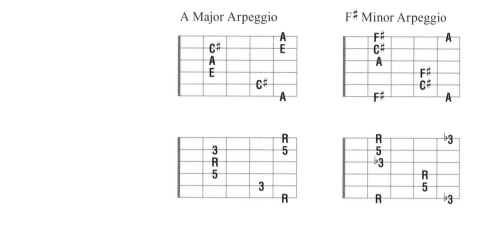

Rhythm 18

(1) and 2   (3) and (4)

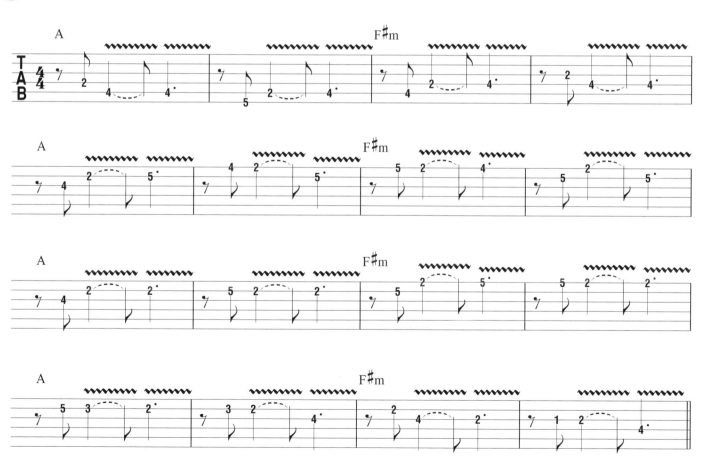

E–to–C#m Solo

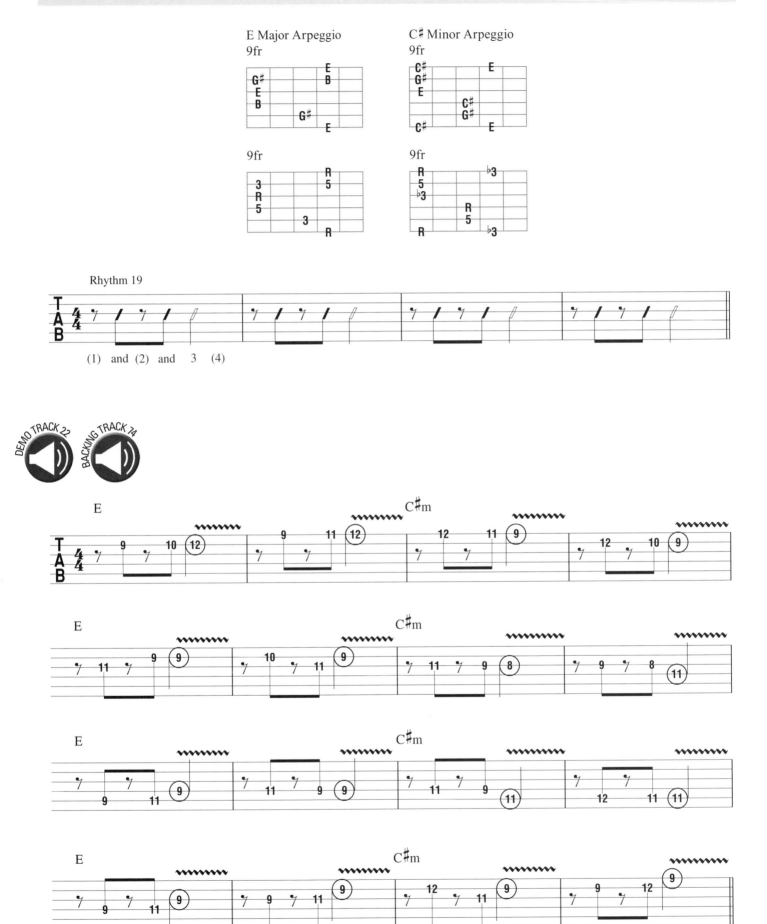

D-to-Bm Solo

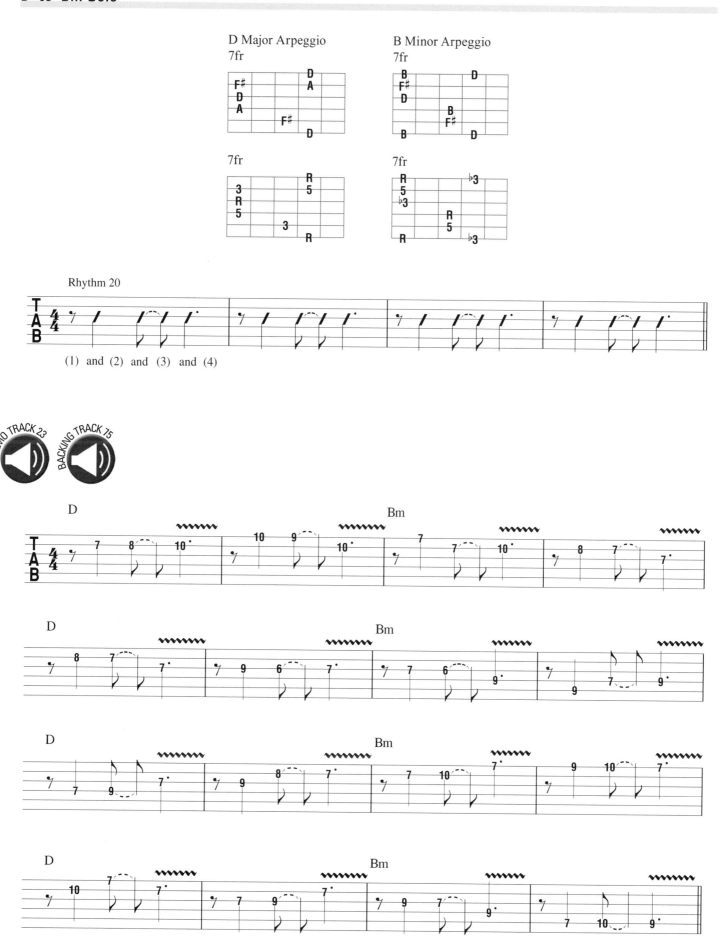

RHYTHM REVIEW

By playing the ten solos found in Chapters 4 and 5, you have added ten rhythmic patterns to your musical vocabulary! Review the patterns by counting them out loud, then go back to any of the previous backing tracks and improvise over them freely, using those rhythms in any way that you choose (i.e., mix and match). Finally, try to combine the patterns with the rhythms from Chapter 3's Rhythm Review. The only limit is your imagination!

Rhythm 11

1 (2) and 3 (4)

Rhythm 12

1 (2) 3 (4) and

Rhythm 13

1 (2) and (3) and (4)

Rhythm 14

1 (2) and (3) 4

Rhythm 15

1 and (2) and (3) (4)

Rhythm 16

(1)   (2)   3   and   (4)   and

Rhythm 17

(1)   and   2   3   (4)

Rhythm 18

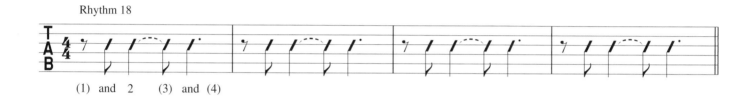

(1)   and   2   (3)   and   (4)

Rhythm 19

(1)   and   (2)   and   3   (4)

Rhythm 20

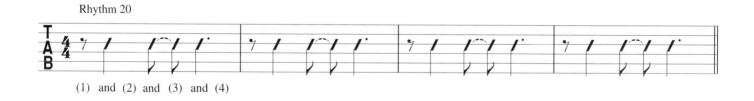

(1)   and   (2)   and   (3)   and   (4)

The following three solos incorporate the new sounds, rhythms, and patterns that you have learned up to this point. Play the solos as eight individual four-bar phrases, playing each phrase along with the backing track, before combining the sections into one complete solo. As you play the solo, notice that each new musical device is labeled for reference.

C-to-Am Solo

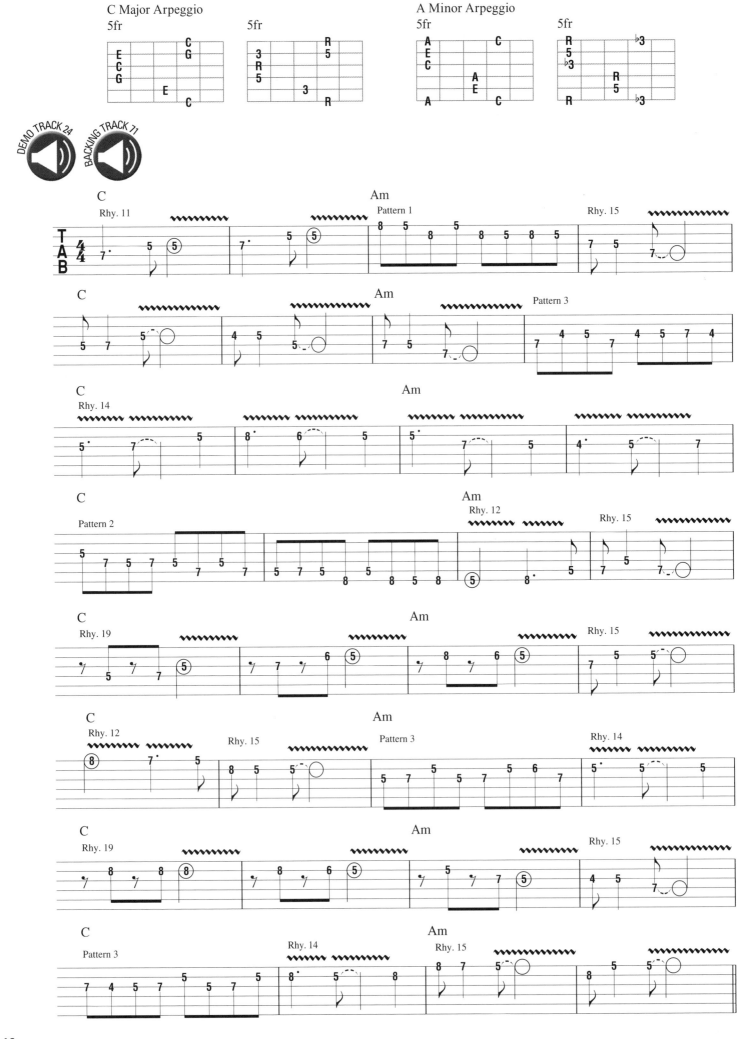

G-to-Em Solo

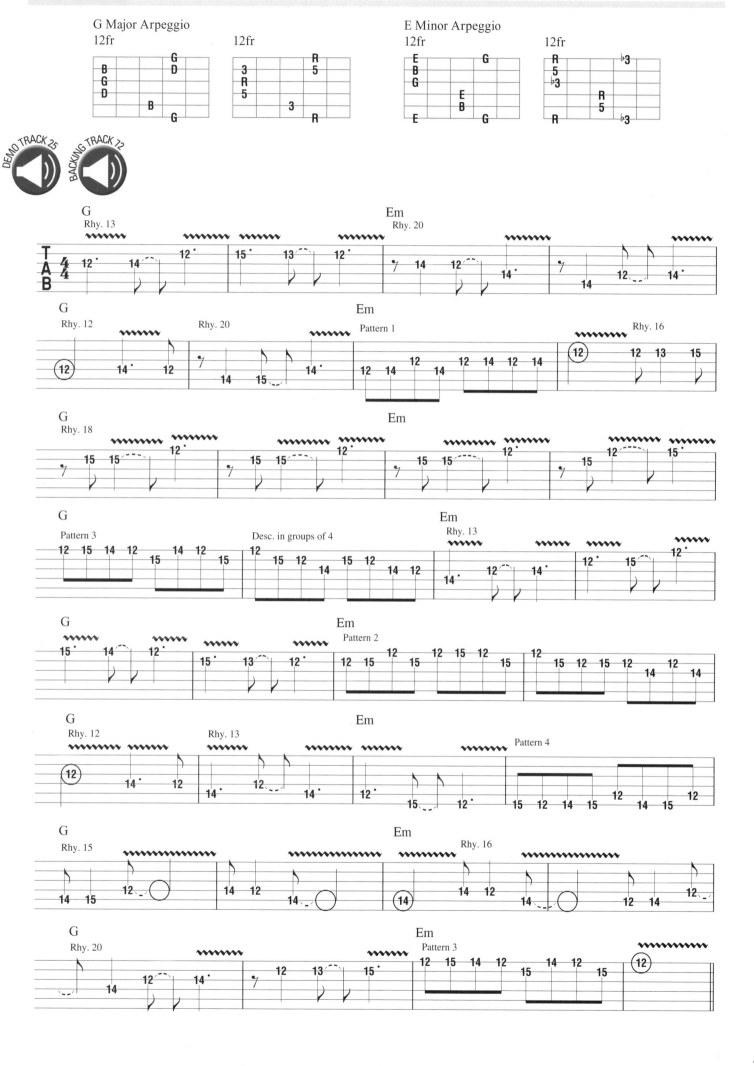

A-to-F#m Solo

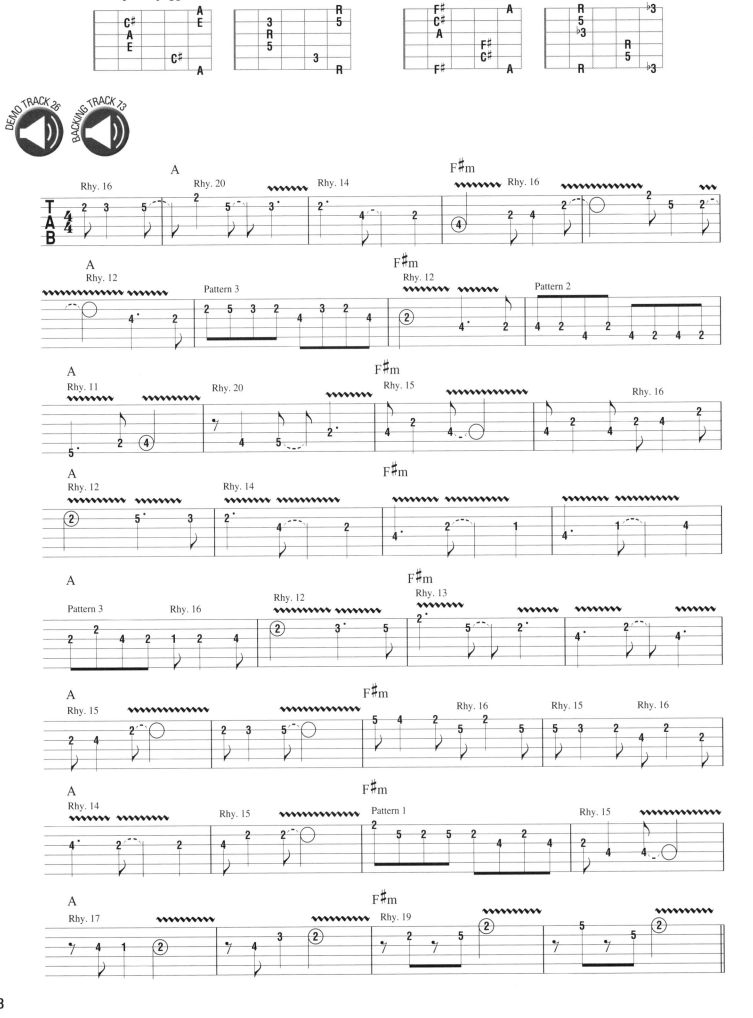

A Major Arpeggio

F# Minor Arpeggio

CHAPTER 6:

EXPANDING THE POSITION WITH SLIDES

In addition to landing on the right notes and learning to build rhythmic phrases, an important aspect of creating interesting guitar solos is the inflections—the way that you play the notes. *Slides* are a great way to give your notes extra flavor. Let's examine three different types of slides.

Shift Slide: Two notes that are connected by a diagonal line indicates that you pick the first note, shift your finger up or down to the next note, then pick the new note to sound it. Shift slides are most commonly used to move between positions along the neck.

Legato Slide: Two notes that are connected by a diagonal line, with a curved line over top, indicates that you pick the first note and slide to the next note without picking it. The slide itself sounds the second pitch.

Grace-Note Slide: A grace note is a note that precedes the intended pitch, giving it extra character or inflection. Grace notes occur very quickly and have no time value; only the destination pitch receives the count. In the following example, notice how the grace notes have no rhythms attached to them. However, be sure to count the main note as beat 1. Think of the slide as the route you are taking to the note you want to play.

The Pentatonic Scale with a Position Shift

A great way to expand the scales that you already know is to utilize the shifting pentatonic scale. When learning this pattern, observe that four of the scale's notes are the same as the one-octave pentatonic scale that you learned in Chapter 1. Initially, you will slide with your middle finger to line up your other fingers perfectly for the remainder of the scale pattern. Study the notes and the fingering below, then play the exercises below them to absorb the new fingering.

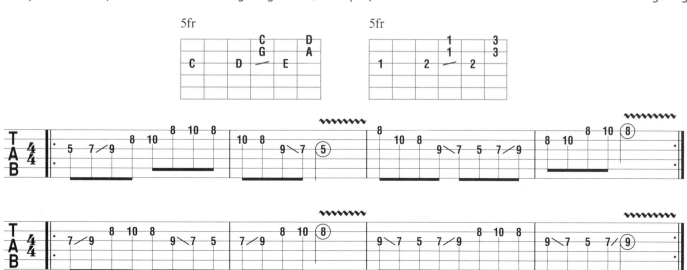

COMMON SLIDING IDEAS

Before presenting new melodic ideas, let's take a look at how each note in our new fingering relates to the chord we are playing over.

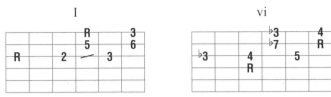

While the most common place to slide is on string 3, sliding on strings 1 and 2 is very useful, as well. Which note you land on depends on how it sits with the chord you are playing over. The following exercise demonstrates sliding notes in both directions. Always remain aware as to whether the note on which the phrase ends feels like tension or release.

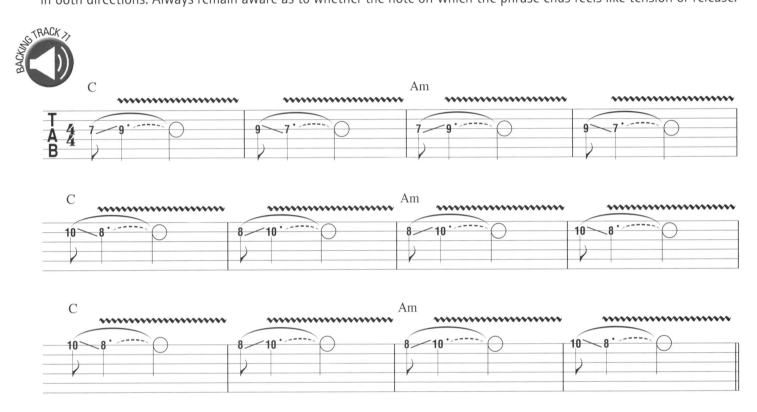

The following examples indicate whether the phrase ends on tension or release. Depending on the situation, the finger that you use for the slides may change. For maximum benefit, start by sliding with your middle finger for the 3rd-string exercise, then with your ring finger. For the 2nd- and 1st-string exercise, slide with your pinky.

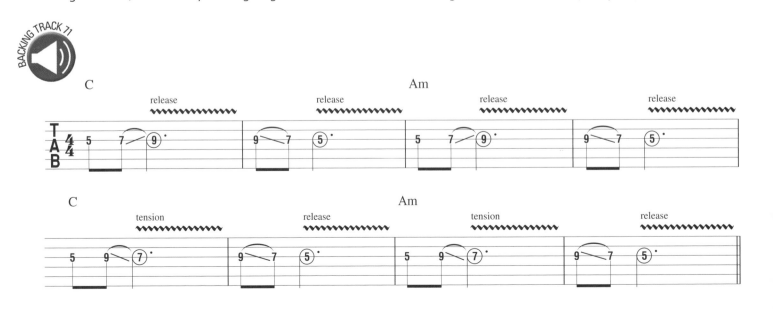

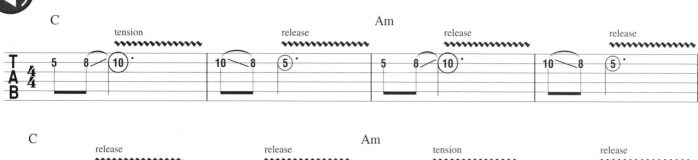

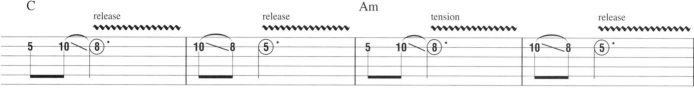

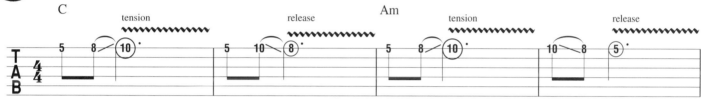

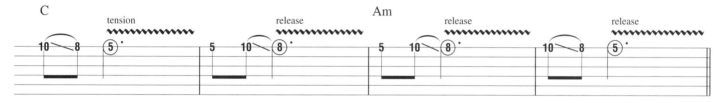

In addition to the ideas that you've just learned, our next exercise will prepare you for one of the most traveled sliding areas on the fretboard. Working this position-shift area will enable you to freely move into a higher register of the scale.

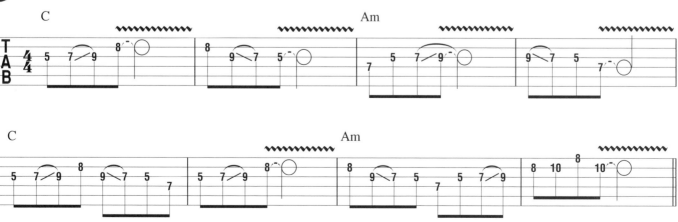

51

SLIDING TO A UNISON NOTE

A great way to utilize our new technique is to play a pitch, then slide into that same pitch (unison note) on a different string. The two basic moves, shown below, involve playing a note from our original one-octave pentatonic scale with your index finger, then sliding into that same note on the adjacent (2nd) string with your ring finger.

This example affords us the opportunity to introduce to our vocabulary two new rhythms that involve sixteenth notes. The first rhythm (measures 5–8) delays the second note's attack by one 16th note, while the second note of the second rhythm (measures 9–12) occurs one 16th note earlier.

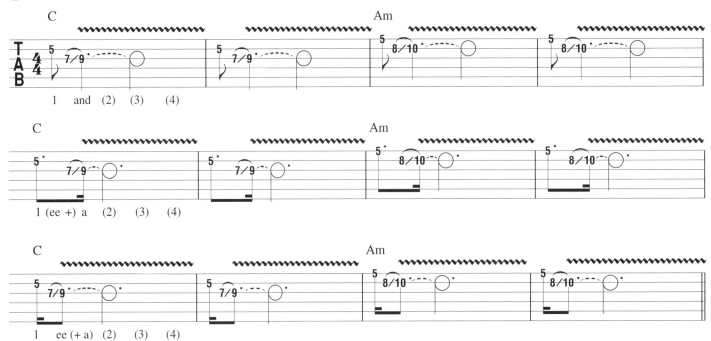

CREATING LONGER PHRASES

In addition to working slides into our musical vocabulary, we also will explore the idea of playing longer phrases. Think of this process as connecting words together to form sentences. Since so much music naturally resolves in four-measure phrases, think of our musical sentences as being four measures long. The words that we fill them with will be the 20 rhythms and melodic patterns that we've used so far.

A great way to begin stringing "words" together is to use a familiar form. *Song forms* are often labeled with rehearsal letters to identify different sections. A very popular song form is AABA. A great example of this form that most people recognize is Beethoven's "Ode to Joy." Take a minute to find it or sing it to yourself. The main theme is constructed of four four-measure phrases that could be thought of as:

A1: The main melodic statement;

A2: The main melodic statement with a resolution;

B: A completely new idea that builds excitement and interest;

A3: A repetition of the main melodic statement with a resolution.

We are going to take this concept and shrink it down to one four-measure phrase, with each section being one measure long and containing two rhythms per line:

Measure 1: Create a melodic idea with one of our rhythms or melodic patterns (A1);

Measure 2: Restate the idea with optional melodic variation (A2);

Measure 3: Introduce a brand new melodic/rhythmic idea (B);

Measure 4: Restate the original idea (with optional melodic variation) to wrap up the phrase (A3).

Of course, every guitar solo will not follow this pattern. Nonetheless, this approach is a great way to give your solos some direction and form, while developing the concept of "telling a longer story." The following examples illustrate this form by using rhythms that are strictly for the sake of study. In the next five solos, we will incorporate the AABA form and sliding techniques that you've just learned. Before you attempt to play the solos, however, try to clap the rhythms to these exercises while counting aloud.

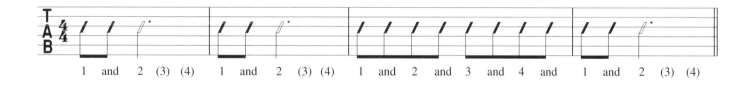

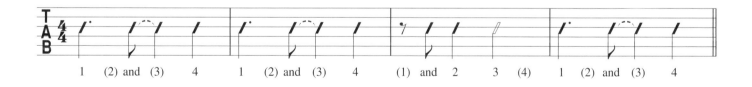

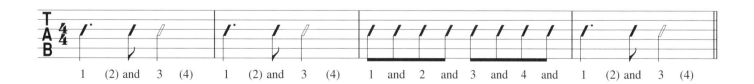

C-to-Am Solo

C Major / A Minor Pentatonic Pattern

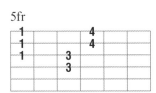 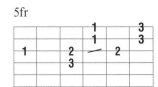 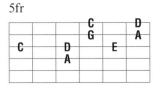

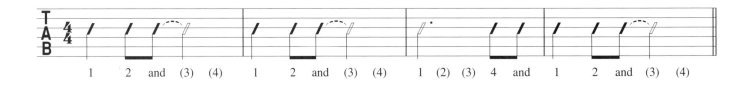

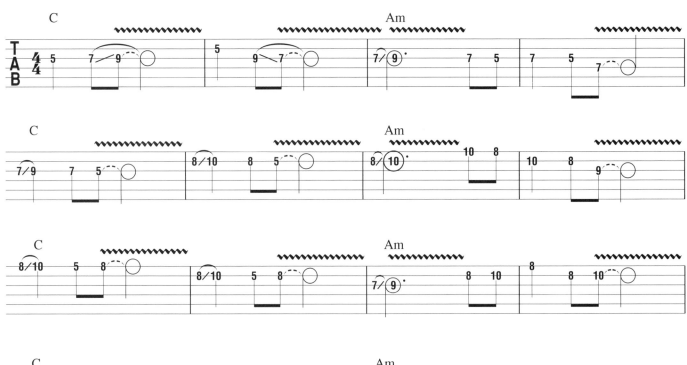

G-to-Em Solo

G Major / E Minor Pentatonic Pattern

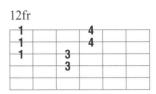
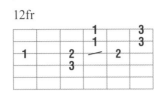
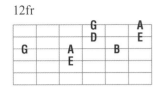

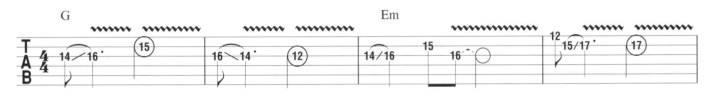

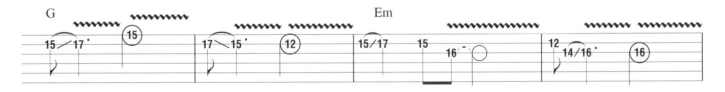

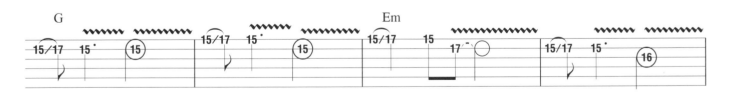

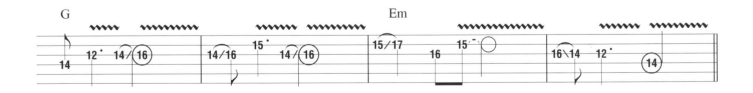

A Major / F# Minor Pentatonic Pattern

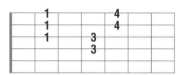 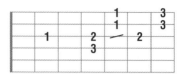 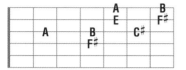

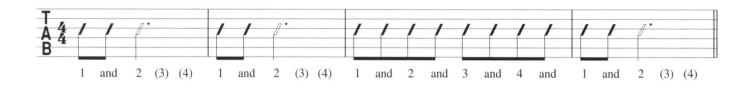

1   and   2   (3) (4)   1   and   2   (3) (4)   1   and   2   and   3   and   4   and   1   and   2   (3) (4)

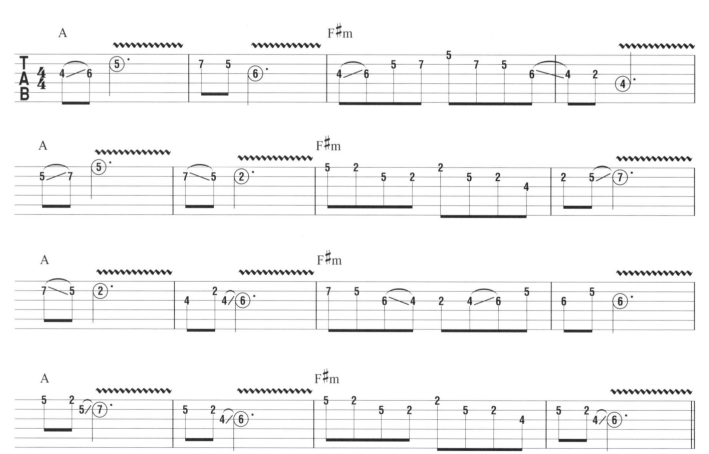

E Major / C# Minor Pentatonic Pattern

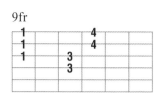
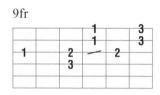
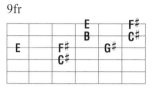

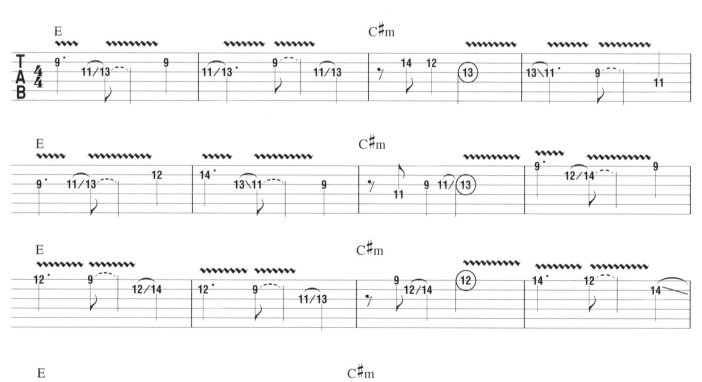

D-to-Bm Solo

D Major / B Minor Pentatonic Pattern

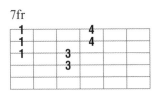 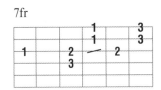 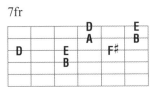

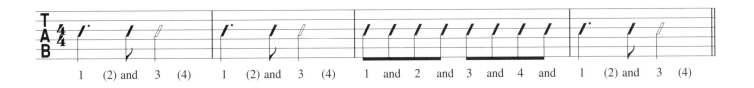

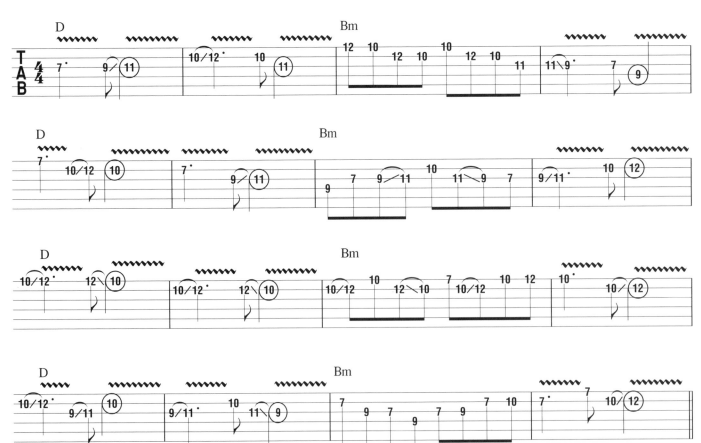

Lower-Octave Pentatonic Scale with a Position Shift

Now that you've gained some experience with slides and have expanded the scale on the top end, let's apply the same concept to the lower octave. For this fingering, you will shift positions on string 5 with your ring finger. All of the notes of this scale are fingered with either your index or ring finger. Study the notes and fingerings below, internalizing the new fingering by practicing the exercises.

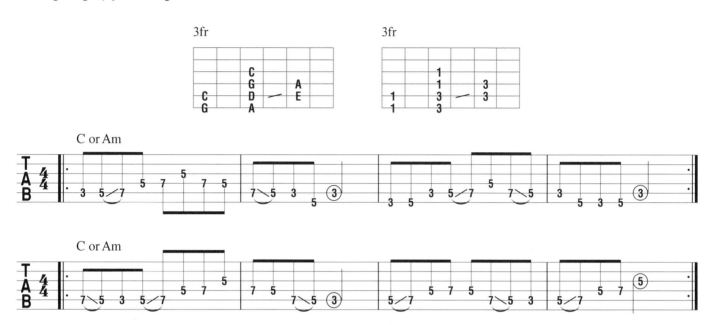

As you learn to use the lower octave of the sliding position, let's add another idea for rhythmic phrasing, ABAB. Simply pick two rhythms and play them back to back, creating a two-measure phrase from which to build melodies. Study each of the five rhythm patterns below, clapping them while counting aloud. These patterns will be the basis for our next five example solos.

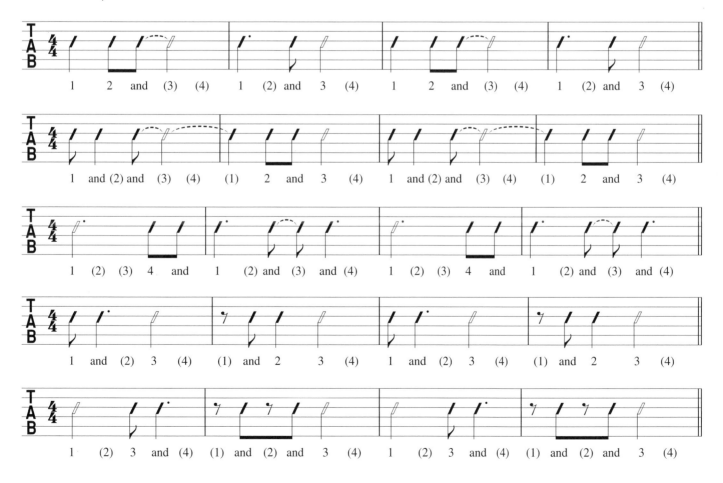

C-to-Am Solo

C Major / A Minor Pentatonic Pattern

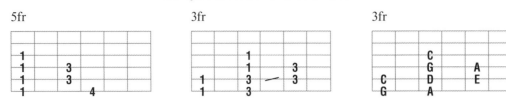

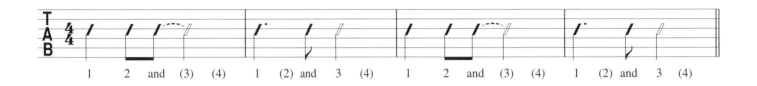

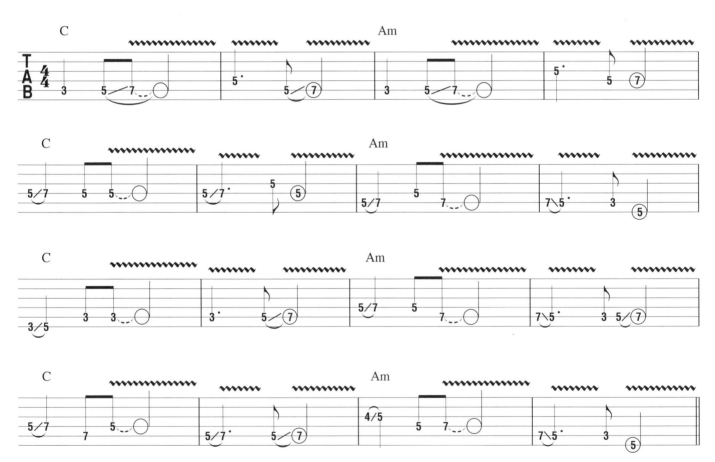

G-to-Em Solo

G Major / E Minor Pentatonic Pattern

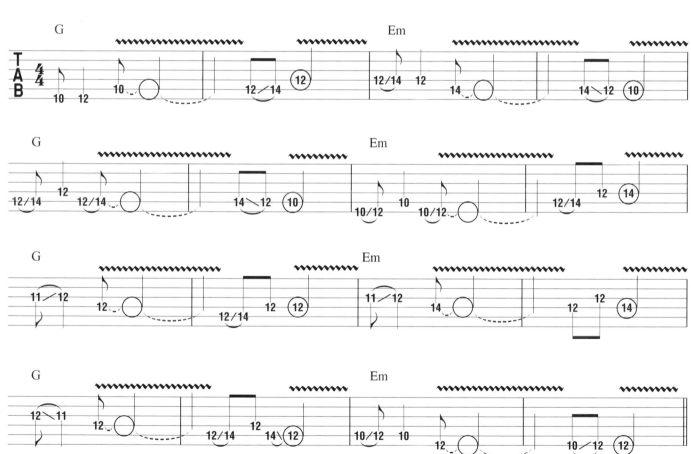

A-to-F#m Solo

A Major / F# Minor Pentatonic Pattern

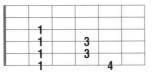 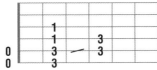 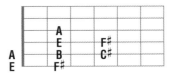

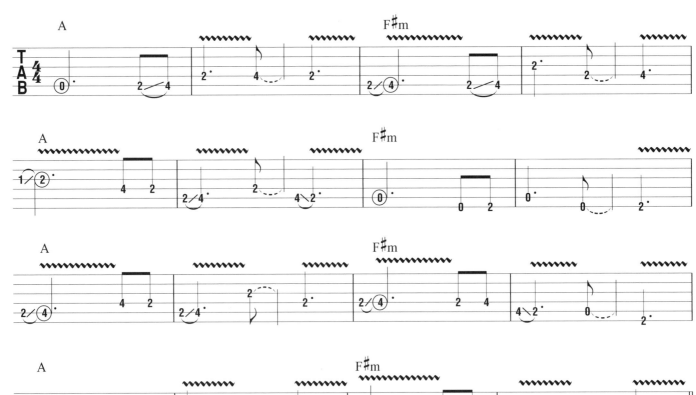

E-to-C#m Solo

E Major / C# Minor Pentatonic Pattern

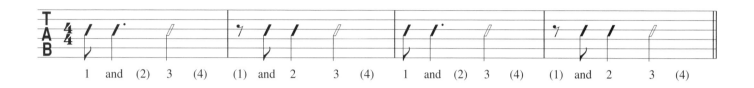

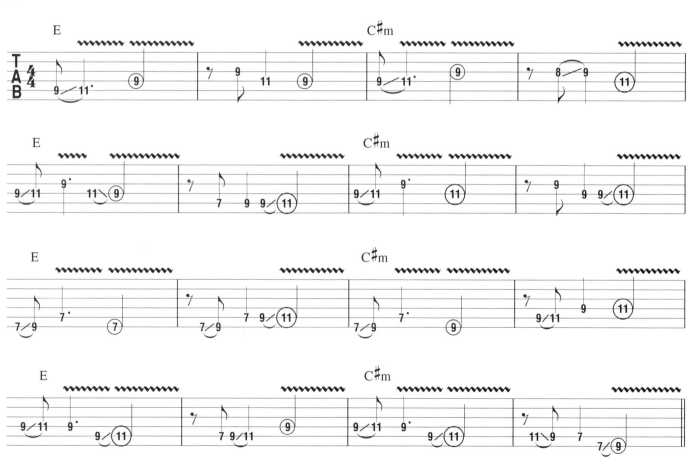

D-to-Bm Solo

D Major / B Minor Pentatonic Pattern

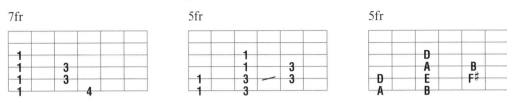

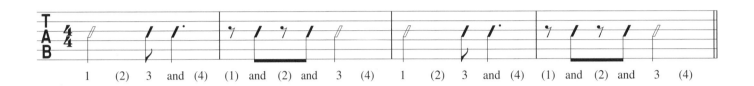

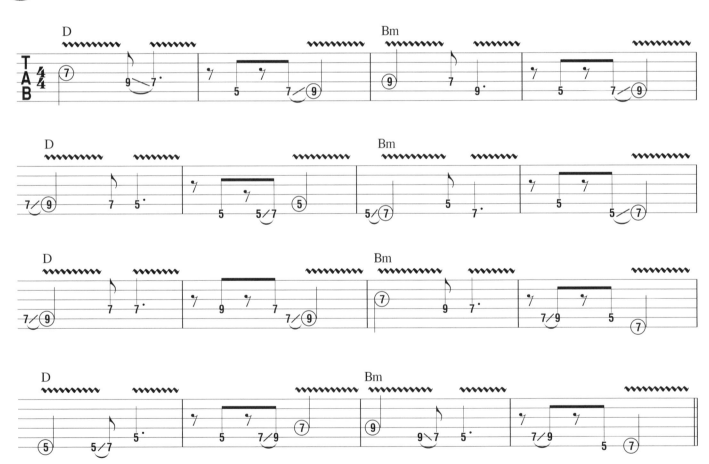

COMBINING BOTH SLIDING POSITIONS

Now that you've worked on each half of the new fingering, it's time to combine them. Utilizing the entire fingering, combined with slides, provides many new options for soloing. Review each half of the scale, then put them together, as shown below.

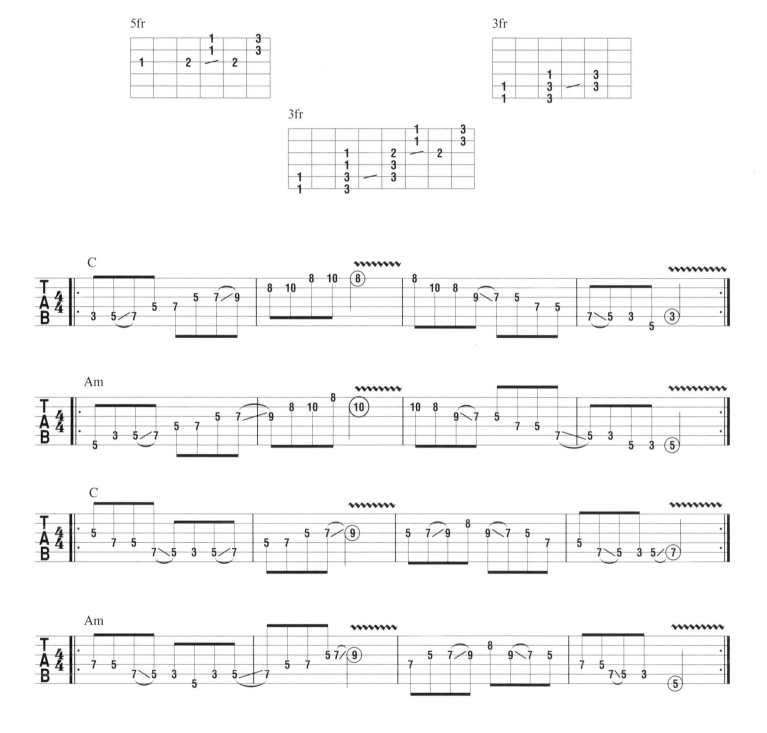

Observe that the full sliding position uses the index and ring fingers for everything but the slide on string 3. Using the middle finger for that slide sets up the upper half of the scale perfectly. As a general rule, practice the scale this way but remember that the ring finger may be used, depending on the situation.

The following solos will use everything that we've explored up to this point in the book, combining all of the scale fingerings and the rhythms with sliding techniques. After learning these examples, make sure to use the backing tracks that are provided on the CD to continue improvising your own solos, drawing from the vocabulary of musical ideas that you have been developing.

C-to-Am Solo

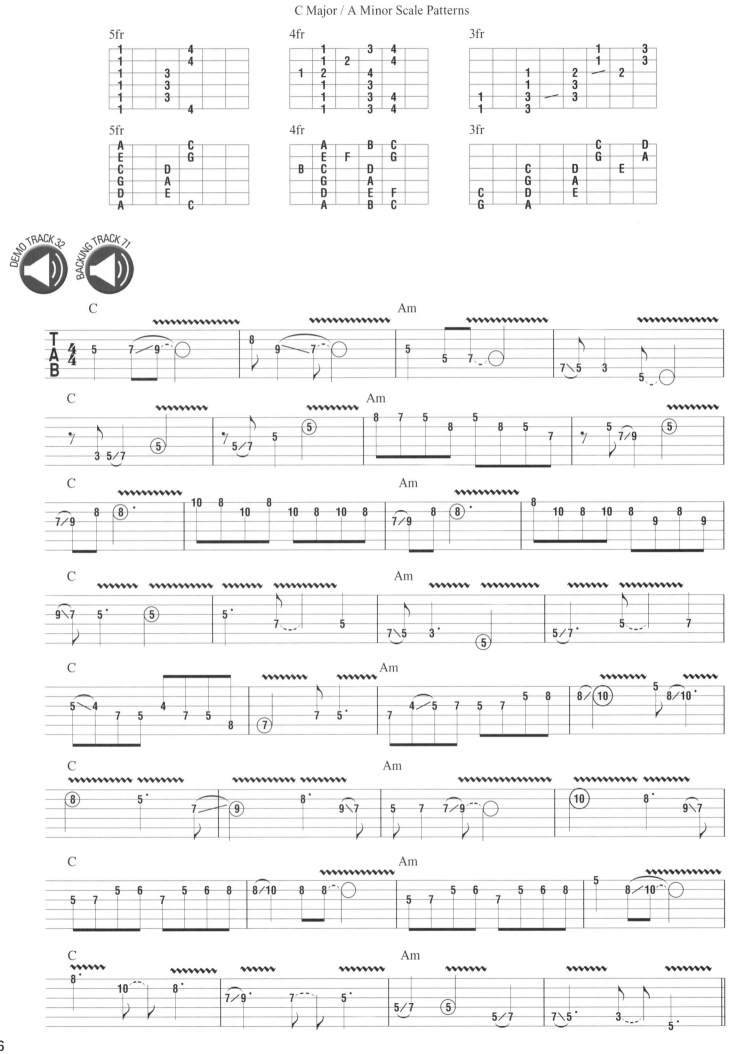

C Major / A Minor Scale Patterns

G-to-Em Solo

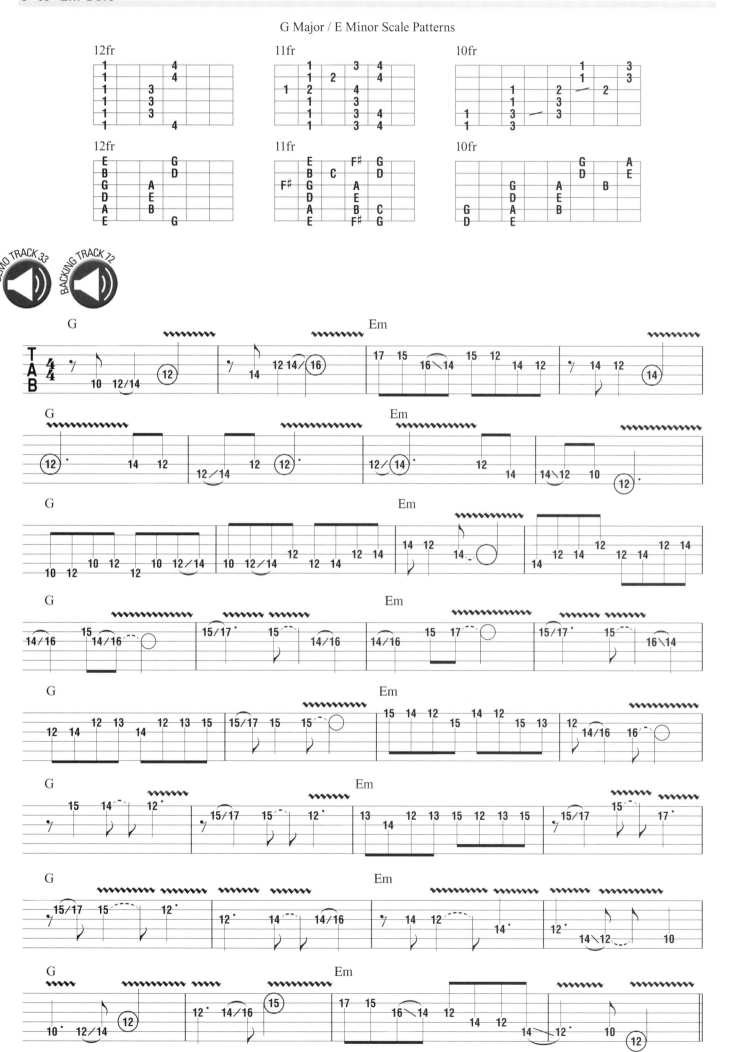

E-to-C#m Solo

E Major / C# Minor Scale Patterns

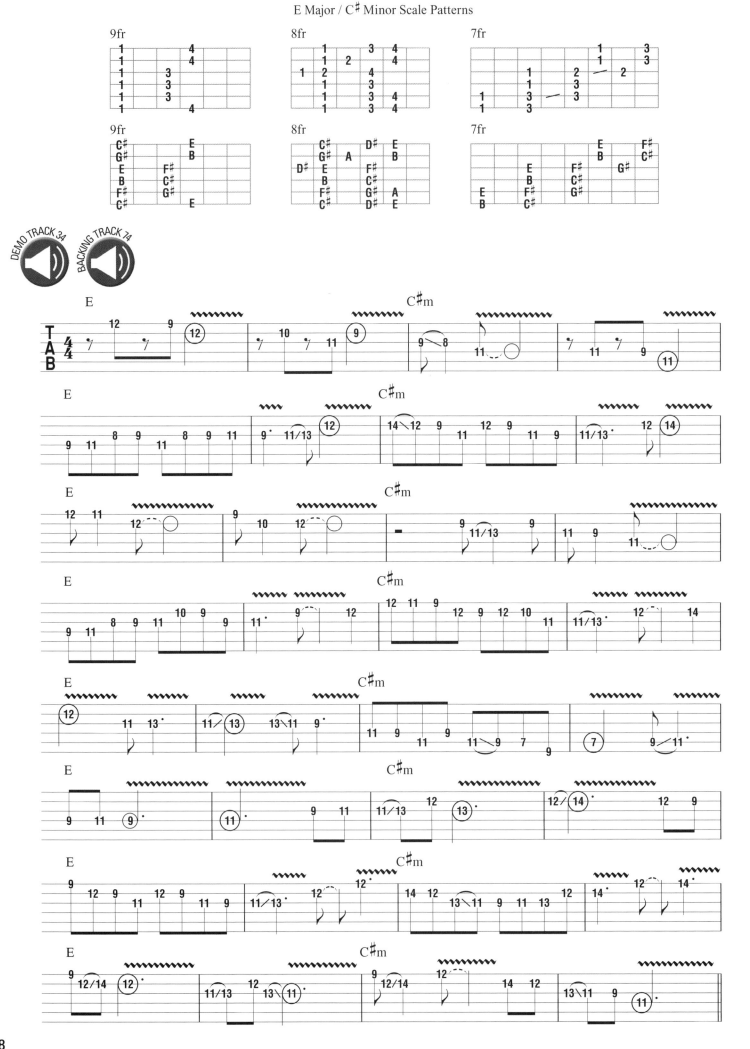

CHAPTER 7:

NEW SCALE POSITIONS

New Major Scale Position

Our next step in creating great guitar solos is to add a completely new fingering position into our arsenal. The major scale can be fingered in many ways on the guitar but history has proven that, in addition to the position that you've already learned, the position below is the second most popular location for guitar soloing. It is common practice for a solo to start in one area and work its way along the neck into different positions, allowing phrases to be played in different registers. Let's begin by playing the C major scale at the 12th fret. Notice that the root of the scale is now on string 2. Practice each of the following exercises slowly to internalize the new pattern.

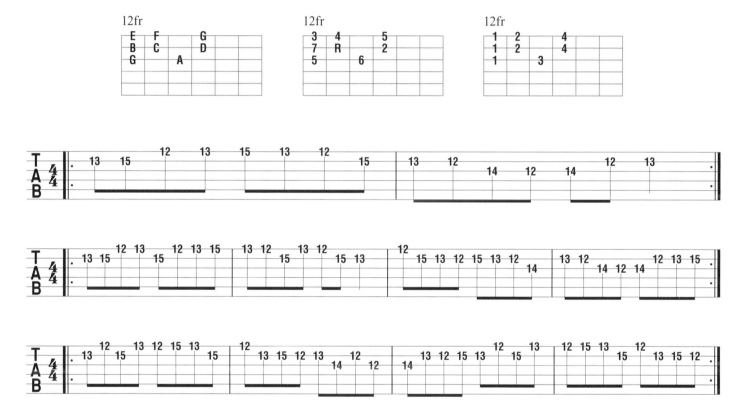

In addition to the scale pattern exercises above, let's take a look at where the strong notes of the scale are located for the I and vi chords. Make these exercises a part of your daily practice routine until you are comfortable with the new fingerings.

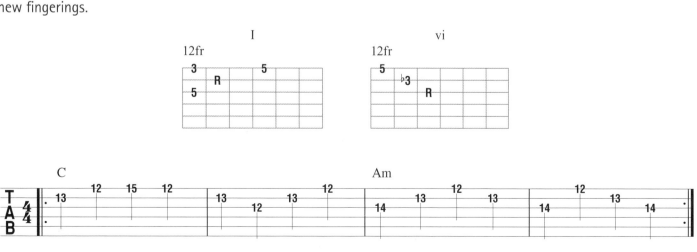

New Pentatonic Position

Just as you learned earlier in the book, our new major scale fingering can be turned into a pentatonic scale by simply removing the 4th and 7th steps of the scale.

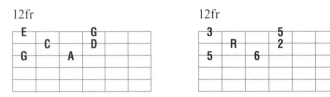

Notice that you can finger this pattern two different ways. Practice both fingerings, as their usage will be situational.

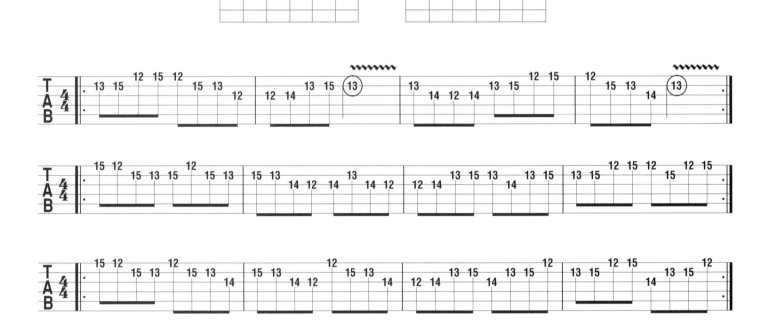

HAMMER-ONS AND PULL-OFFS

Another extremely useful pair of techniques to employ when soloing are the *hammer-on* and the *pull-off*. Much like slides, these slurs can be used to add a new inflection to your notes. A hammer-on is notated by connecting two numbers with a slur marking, as shown below, with the second number being greater than the first. Pick the first note, then "hammer on" to the second note by quickly hammering down your finger behind the fret that you intend to play, without picking it again. The hammer sounds the note. As with slides, a note that is not connected to a rhythm is a "grace hammer"—only the second note receives the count, and the grace note is thought of as an inflection that precedes the destination note. To become acquainted with the technique, practice the following exercise:

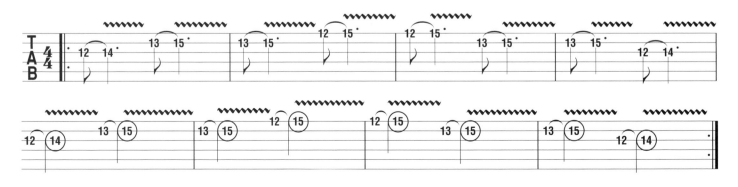

Pull-offs can be thought of as the opposite of a hammer-on. Pull-offs are written the same way, but the first number will be greater that the second. A pull-off indicates that you pick the first note and flick your finger towards the floor to sound the second note, without picking it again.

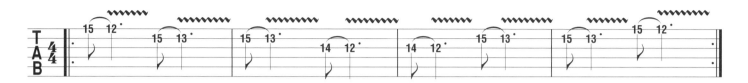

A useful benefit of these techniques is the additional fluidity and speed that you can achieve by not sounding every note with the pick. Play the following exercises, which include the new fingering, as well as hammer-ons and pull-offs, taking your time to insure that you are only picking where indicated. Add these exercises to your daily practice routine.

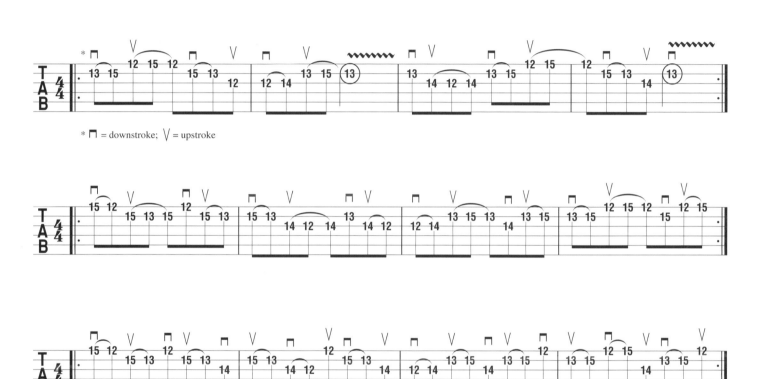

In our next group of solos, we will be adding a fourth note to our rhythmic phrases, as well as adding hammer-ons and pull-offs to our arsenal. To facilitate the absorption of more rhythmic patterns, we'll use the ABAB format that you learned in the previous chapter. As before, count the rhythms aloud before learning the example solos.

C-to-Am Solo

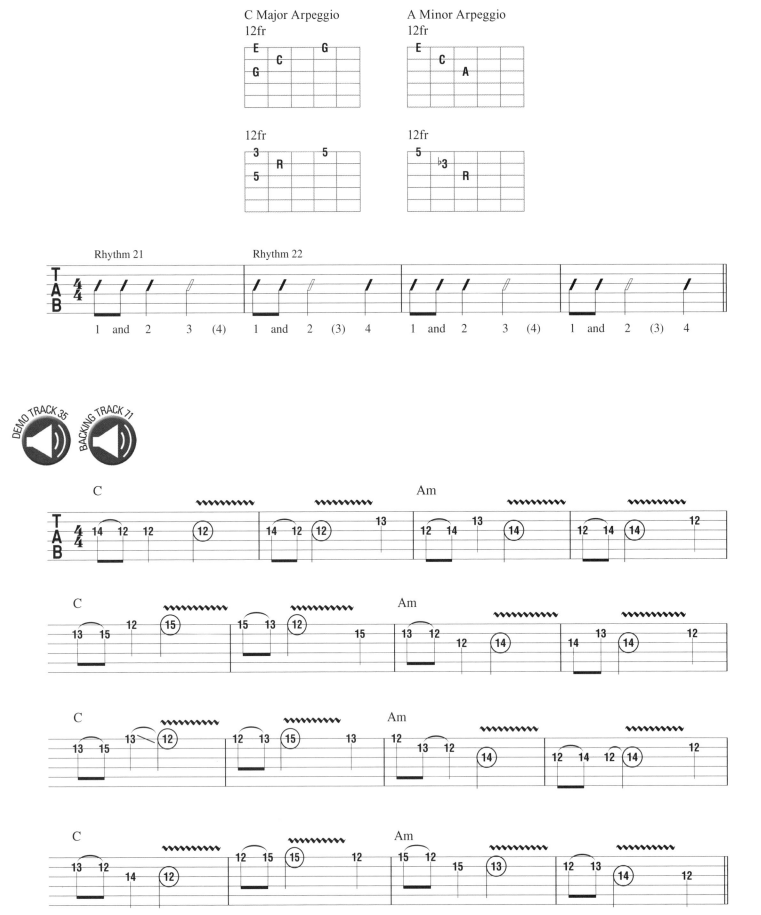

G-to-Em Solo

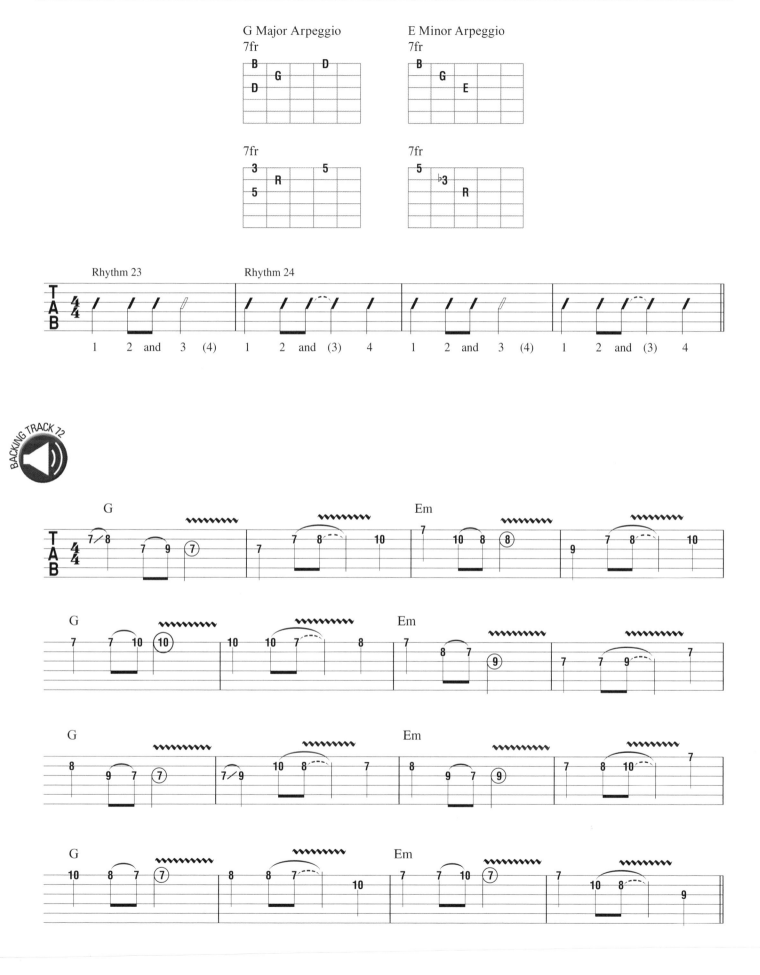

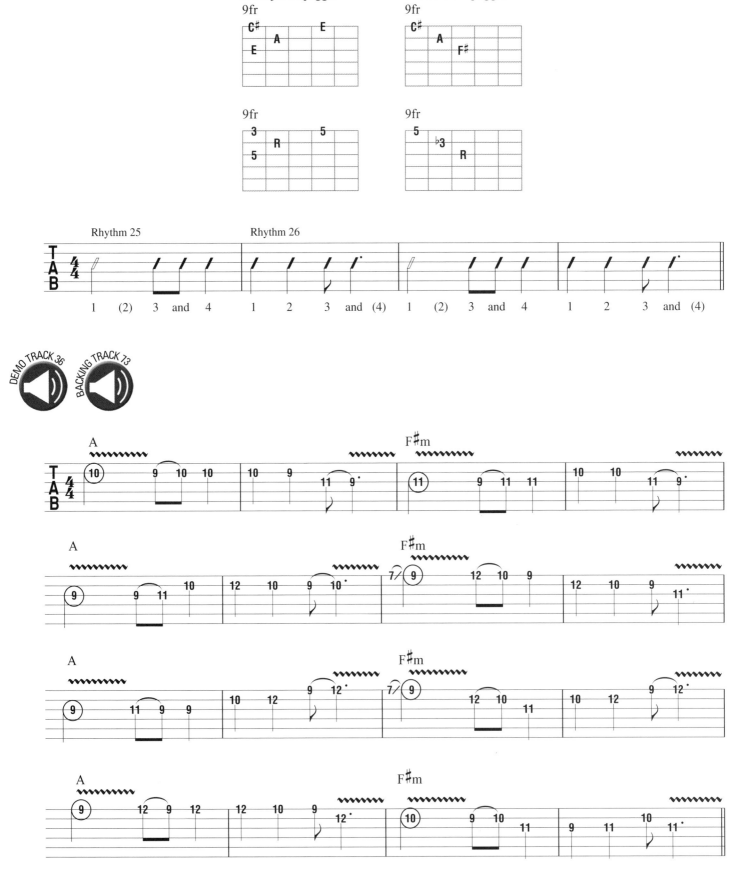

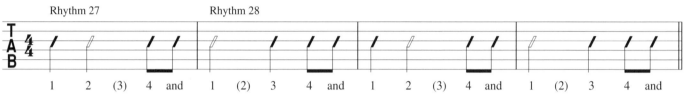

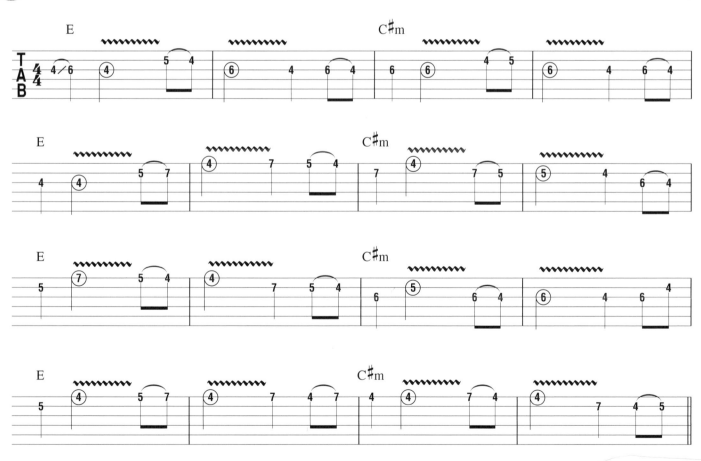

D-to-Bm Solo

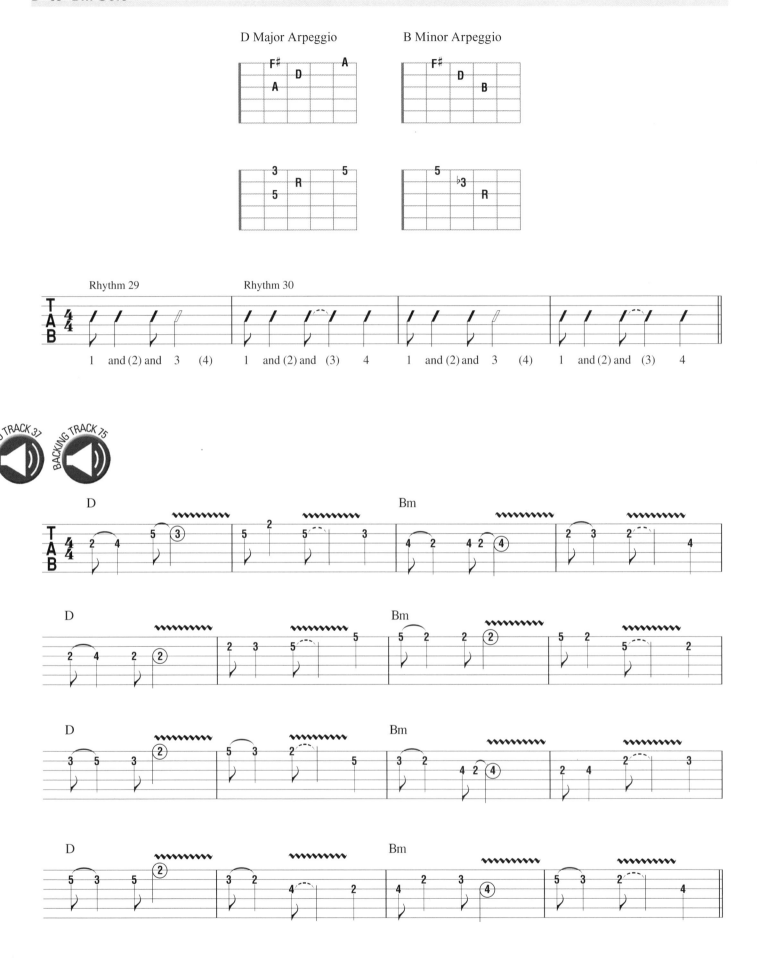

CHAPTER 8:

NEW LOWER-OCTAVE SCALE POSITIONS

New Lower-Octave Major Scale Position

Now that you've got your feet wet with the upper-octave of our new position, let's apply the same ideas to the lower octave. Work slowly through the new fingerings and exercises below, adding them to your daily practice routine.

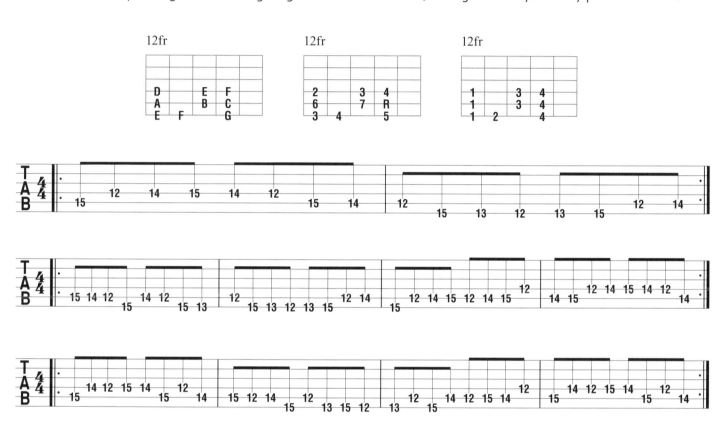

As we did with the upper portion of the scale, examine where the strong notes are located for the I and vi chords. Along with learning fingerings, playing this exercise will continue to reinforce the sound of each chord.

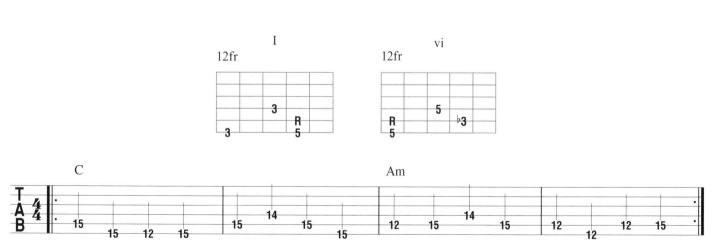

New Lower-Octave Pentatonic Position

Once again, removing the fourth and seventh degrees of the scale yields the familiar sound of the major pentatonic scale. As you practice these exercises, always keep in mind as to where the scale's root is located.

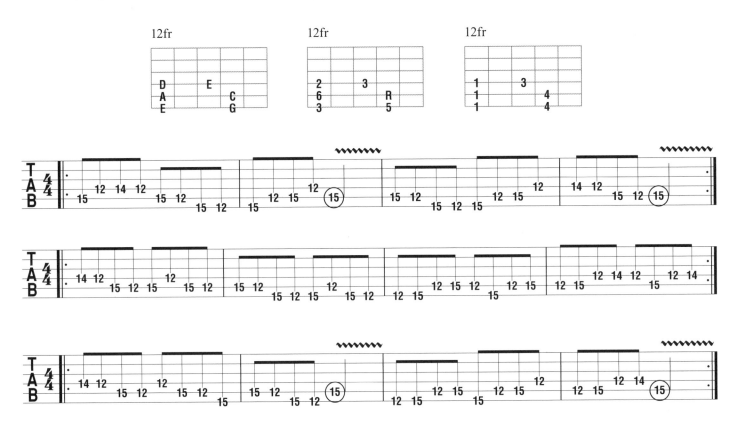

As you learn these new fingerings, try to play the exercises with hammer-ons and pull-offs. By doing so, you will add new meanings to the vocabulary that you already possess.

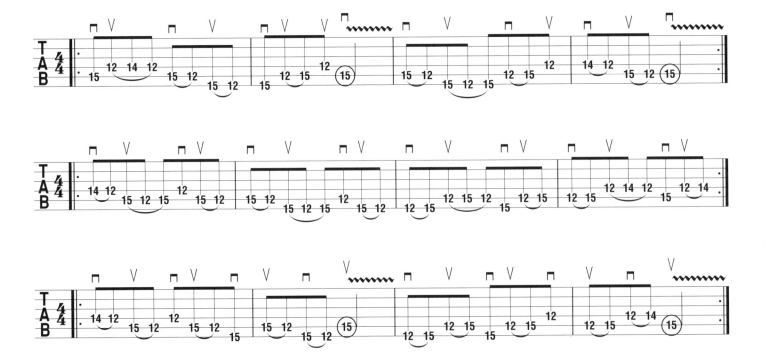

C-to-Am Solo

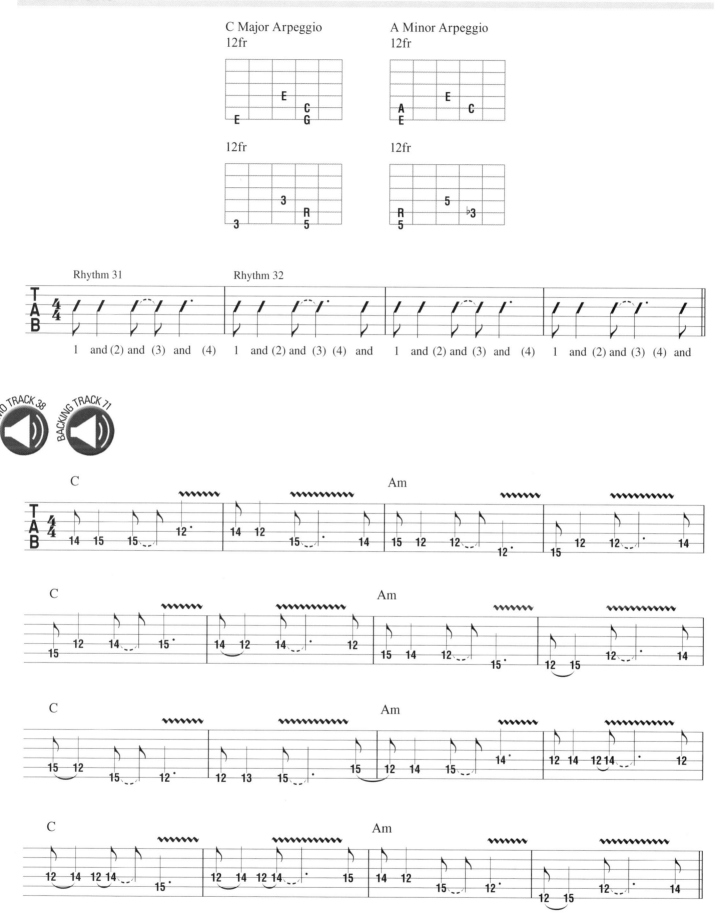

G-to-Em Solo

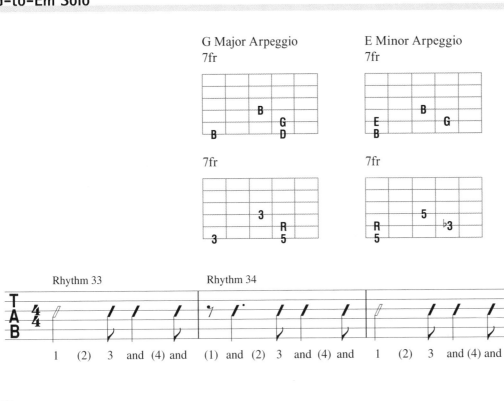

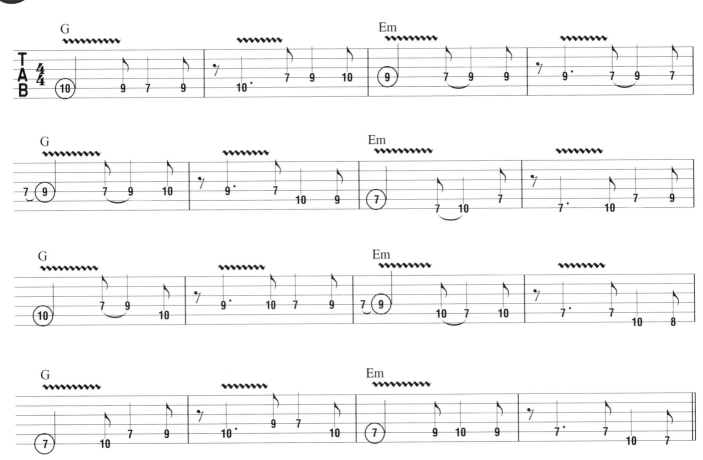

A-to-F#m Solo

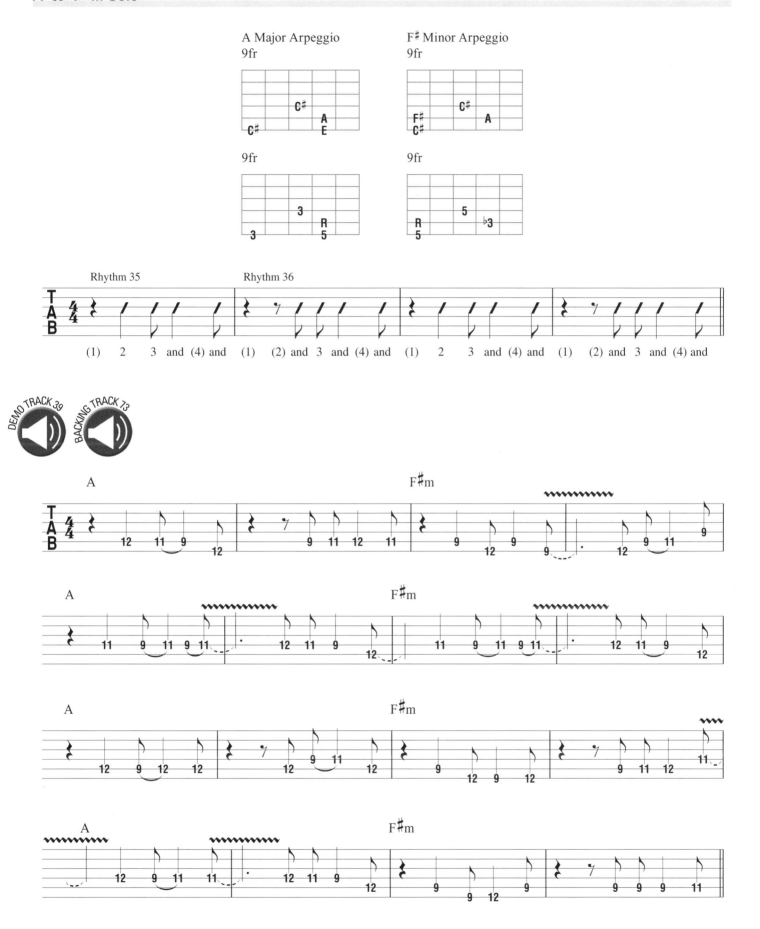

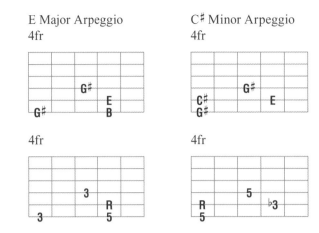

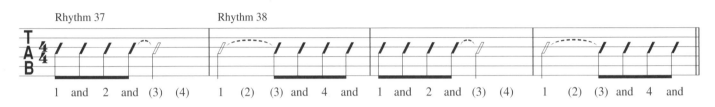

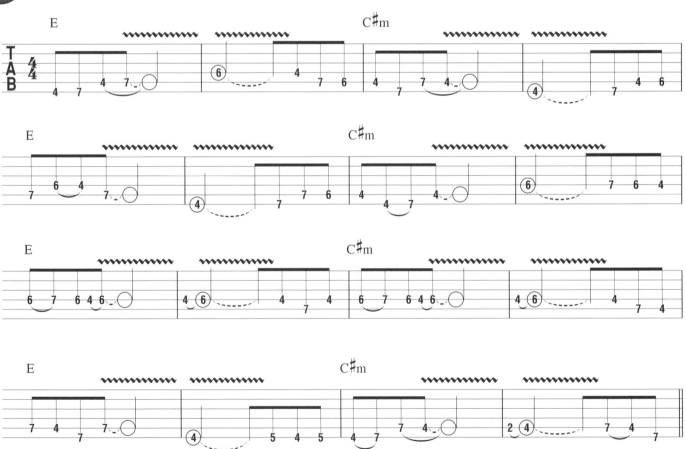

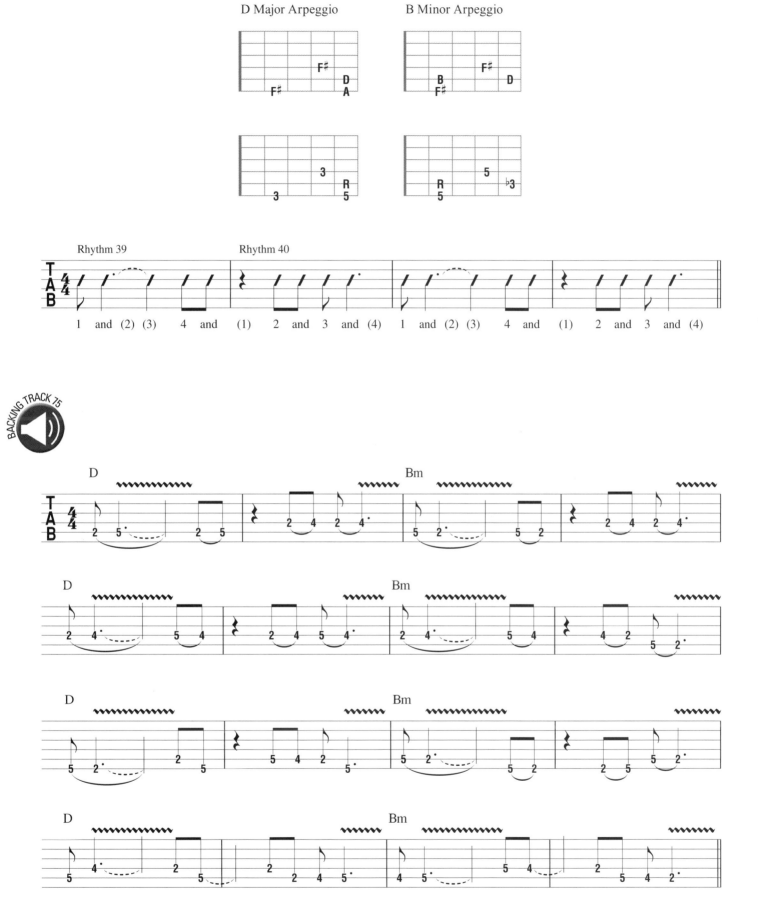

RHYTHM REVIEW

This time around, we've pushed the envelope and introduced 20 new, four-note rhythm patterns. As before, count each pattern aloud before going back to the backing tracks to improvise over them. Feel free to mix and match the new rhythms with the three-note rhythms from previous chapters.

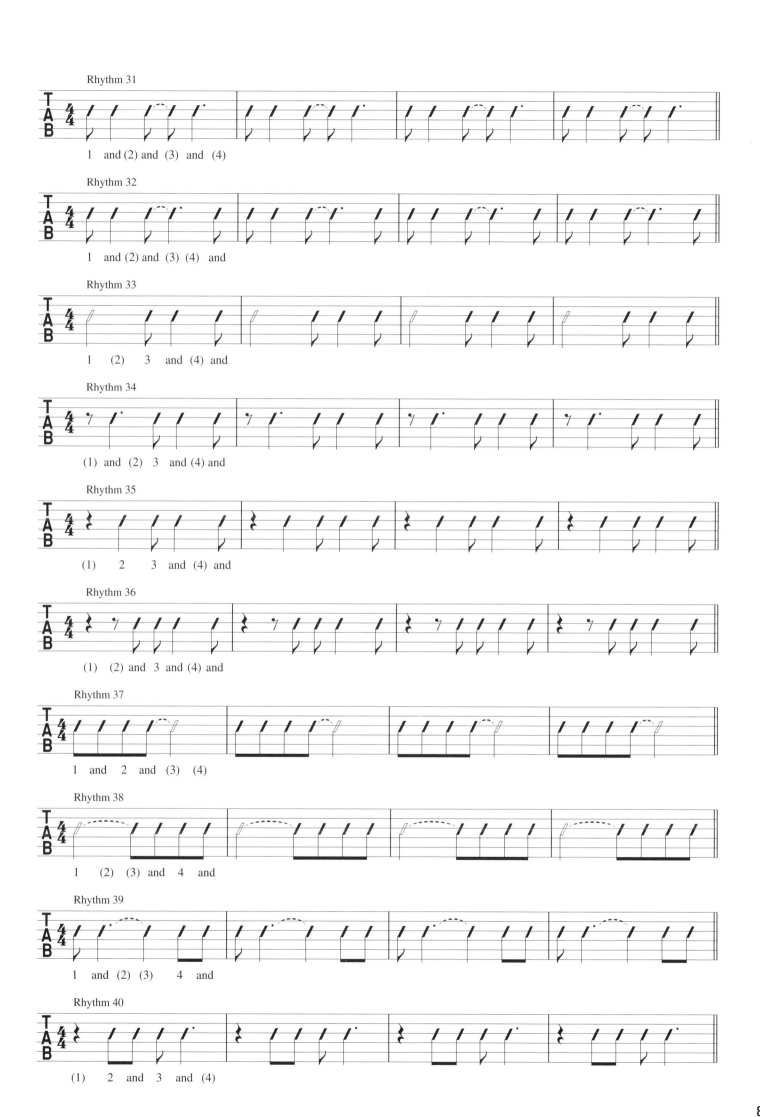

Rhythm 31

1 and (2) and (3) and (4)

Rhythm 32

1 and (2) and (3) (4) and

Rhythm 33

1 (2) 3 and (4) and

Rhythm 34

(1) and (2) 3 and (4) and

Rhythm 35

(1) 2 3 and (4) and

Rhythm 36

(1) (2) and 3 and (4) and

Rhythm 37

1 and 2 and (3) (4)

Rhythm 38

1 (2) (3) and 4 and

Rhythm 39

1 and (2) (3) 4 and

Rhythm 40

(1) 2 and 3 and (4)

CHAPTER 9:

COMBINING BOTH OCTAVES

Now that you've gained some experience with both octaves of our new position, it's time to utilize both of them with some new example solos. The following solos incorporate all of the techniques that you've learned so far. Before playing the solos, work on these exercises to help you visualize the entire new pattern as one fingering:

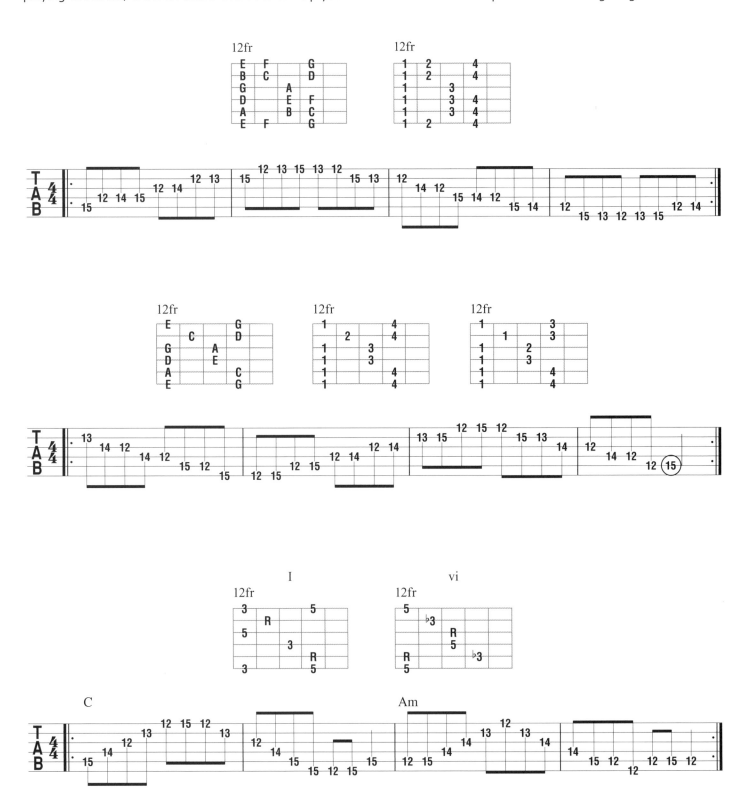

C-to-Am Solo

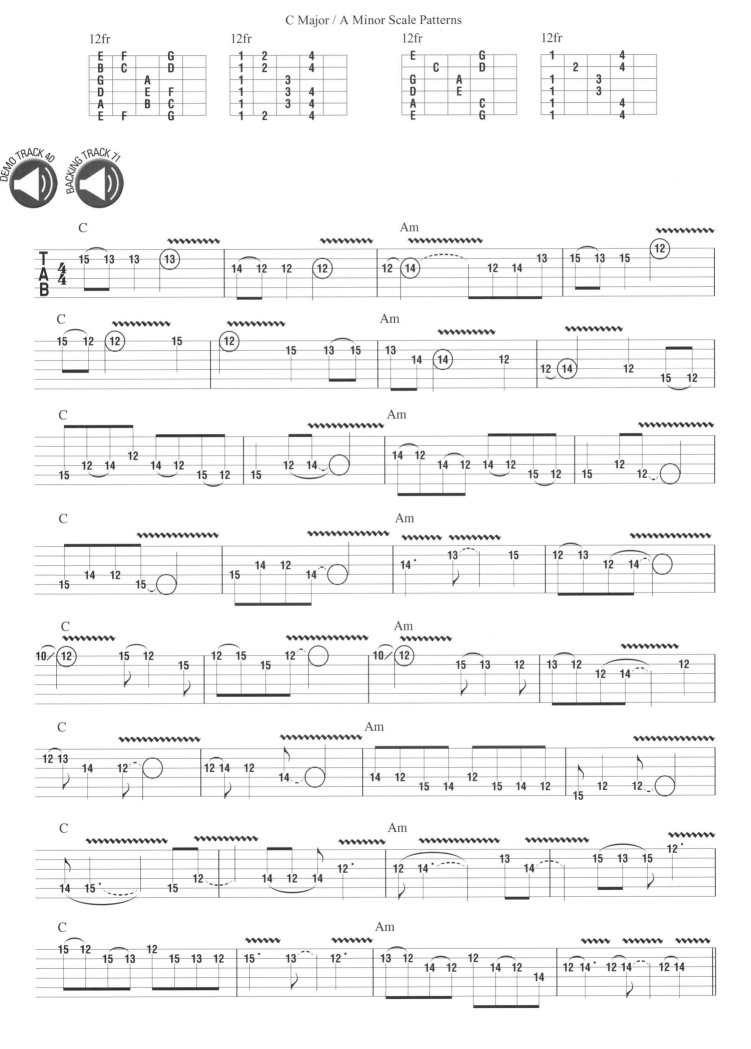

G-to-Em Solo

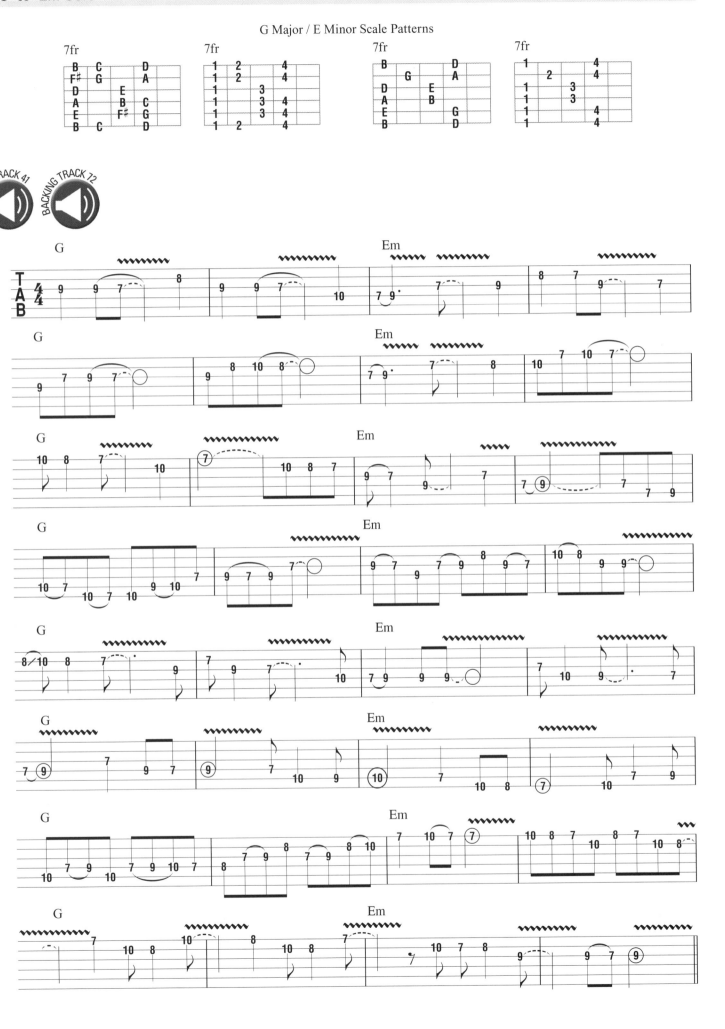

D-to-Bm Solo

D Major / B Minor Scale Patterns

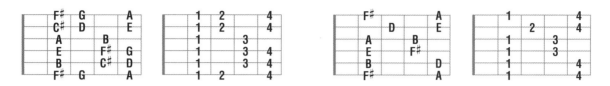

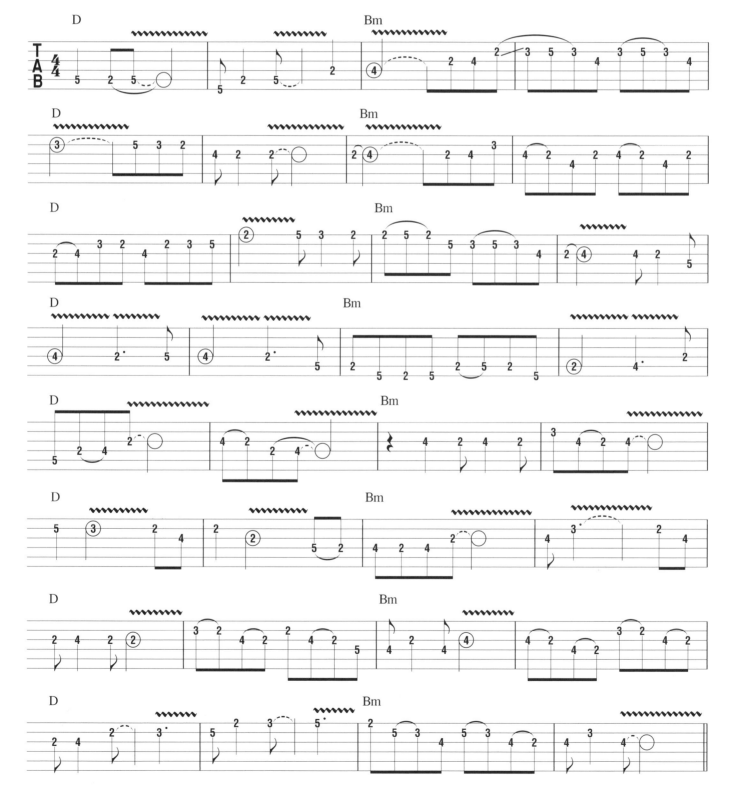

CHAPTER 10:

LEARNING THE SOUND OF IV AND V

In addition to the two main tonalities that we've been focusing on (I and vi), the chords built from the 4th and 5th degrees of the major scale certainly are the most used in all styles of music. Chord progressions using the I, IV, V, and vi can be found throughout the entire history of music and are still being used today. Let's examine the sound of each new chord by focusing on where the chord tones lie within the fingerings that you've already been using. Practice the following exercises, absorbing both the new sounds and the fingerings of the arpeggios.

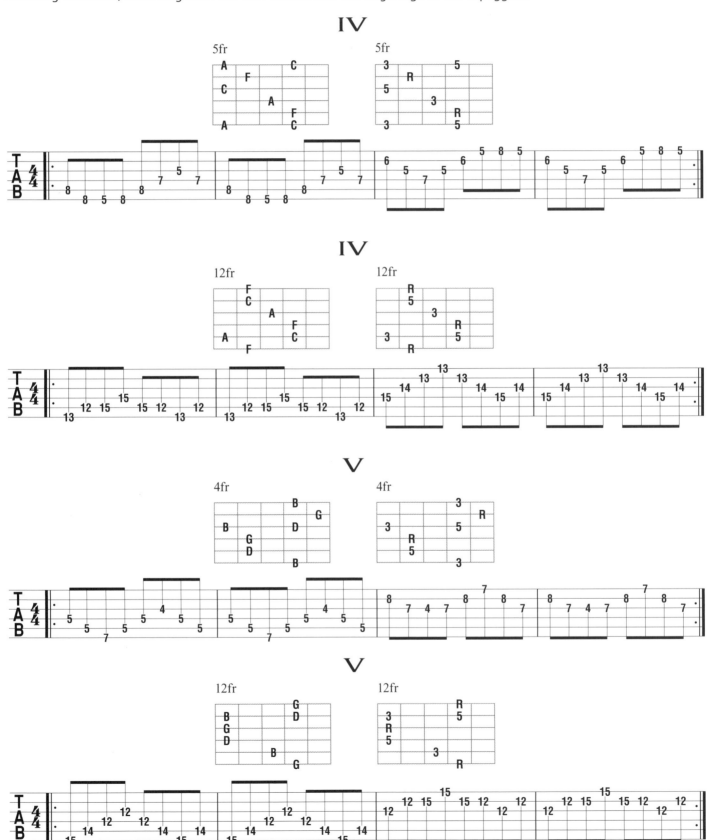

COMBINING I, IV, V, AND VI

The following exercises arpeggiate each of the four chords, separating each position into its upper and lower octave. Practicing these exercises will help you to hear the sound of each chord, which will, in turn, help you to feel which notes to resolve to as you improvise over them. Keep these exercises in your daily practice routine, as they also will reacquaint you with the first position that you learned.

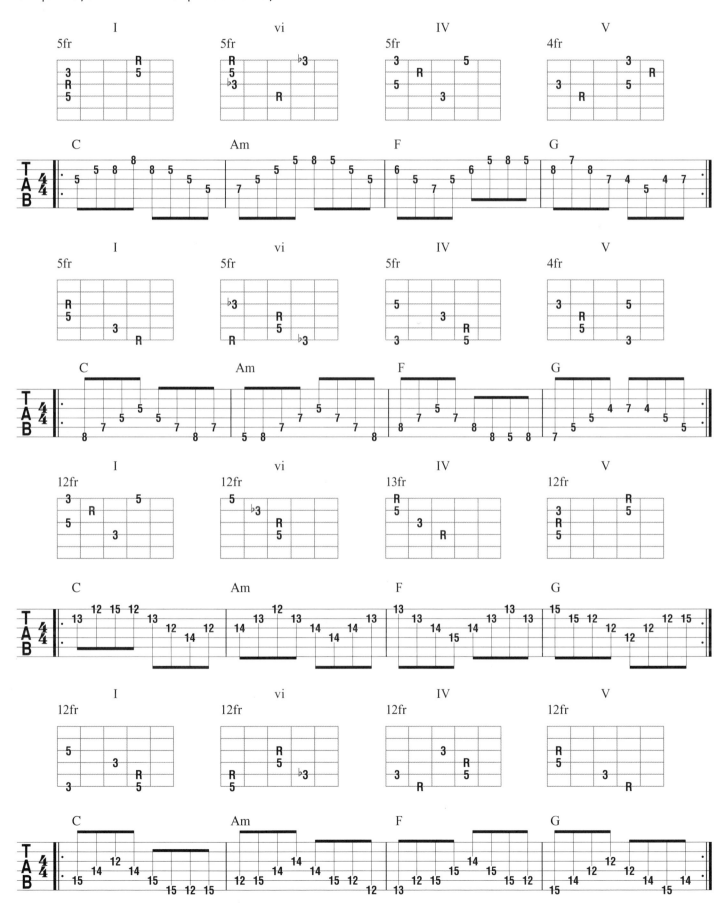

The next five example solos use chord progressions that contain our new chords. The first two lines use the first fingering that you learned, while the last two lines utilize our newest fingering. As before, start by counting and clapping the rhythmic phrase that the solo is based on. Next, learn each line, one at a time, before improvising freely over the backing track while using the rhythmic phrase as a guide. Each arpeggio is shown at the top of each page as a reference point for the strongest notes of each chord change. Keep in mind that the main goal is to continue using your ear as a guide as to which notes to land on.

Additionally, another device that is used to give the solos direction is the ABAC song form. Each of the solos follow this pattern. You may think of this form as a question and answer, with a different answer the second time the question is asked.

C–F–G–Am Solo

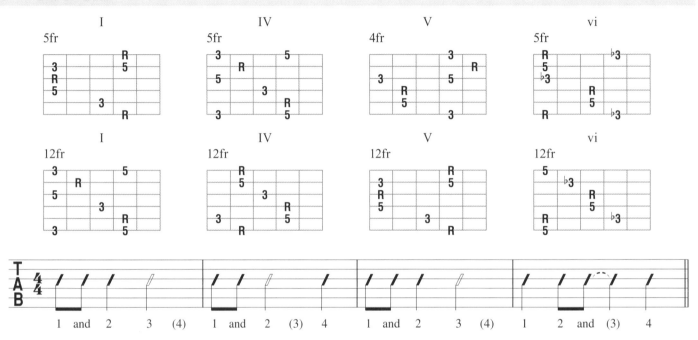

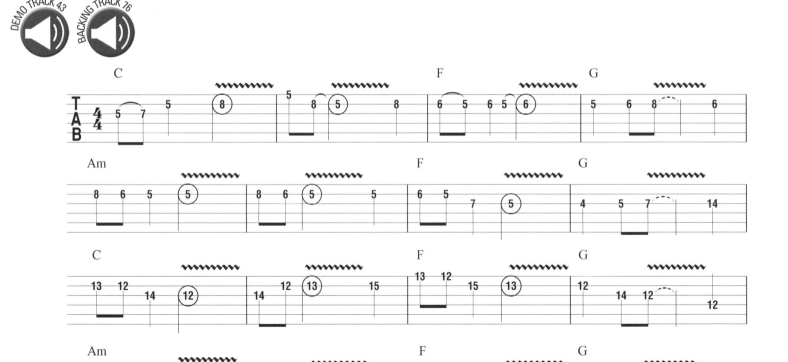

G–C–D–Em Solo

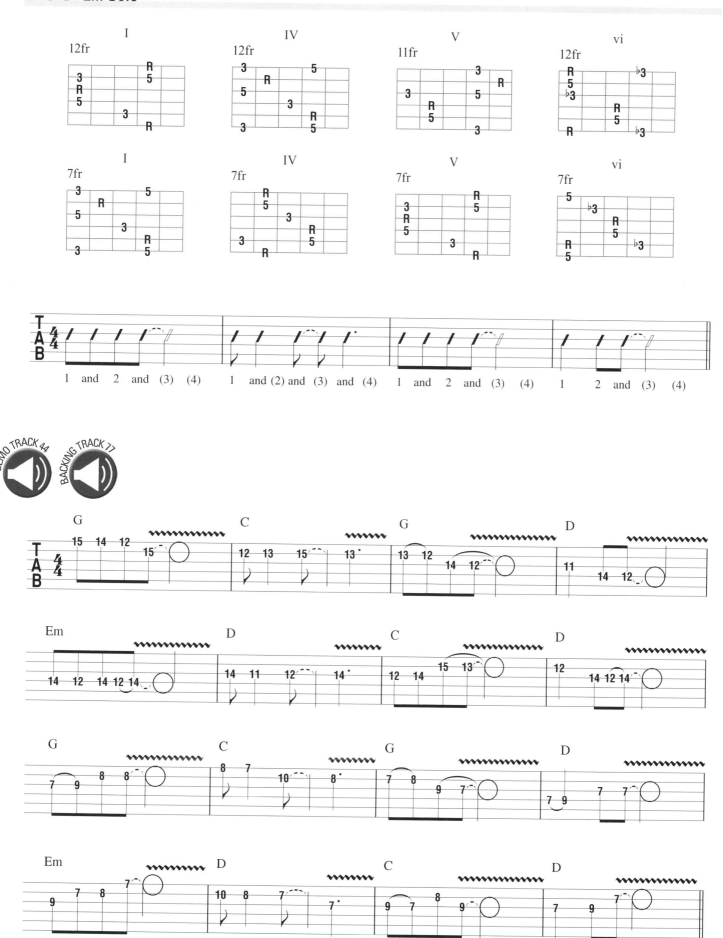

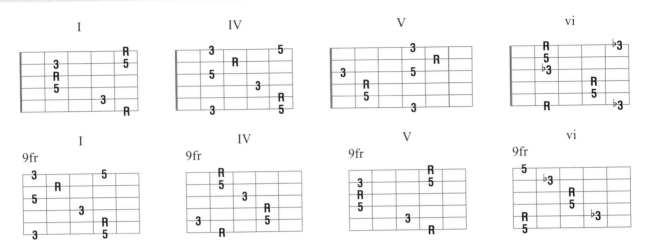

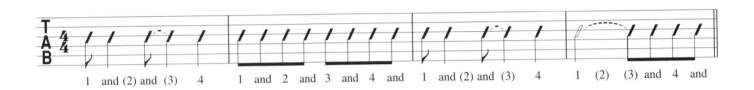

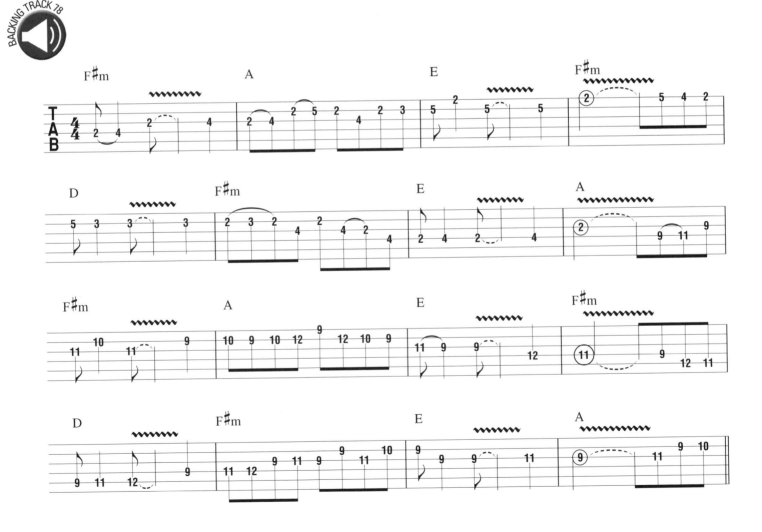

E–A–B–C#m Solo

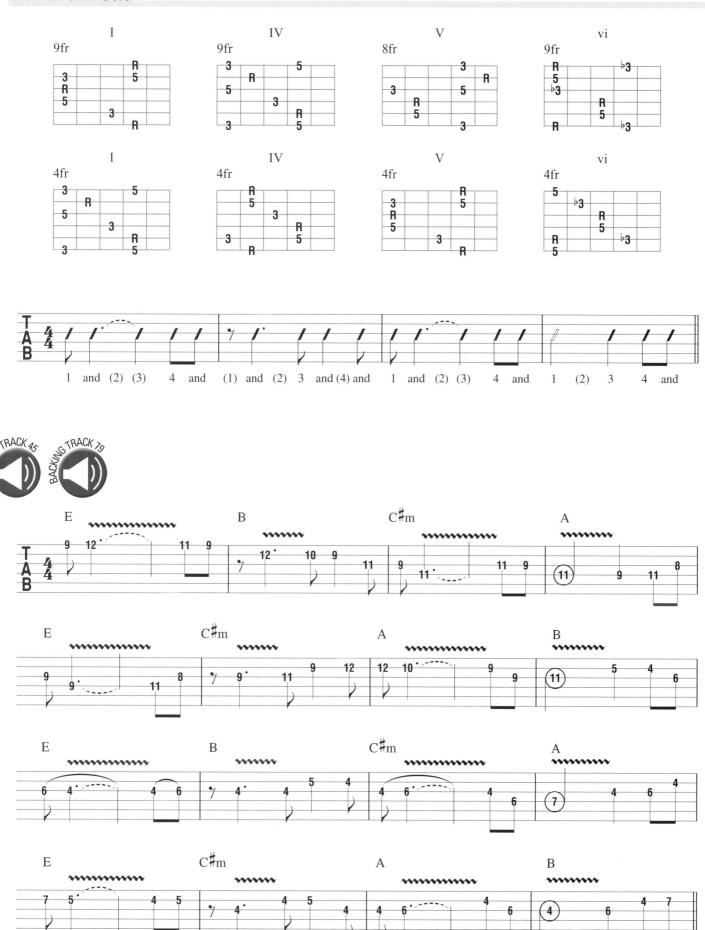

D–G–A–Bm Solo

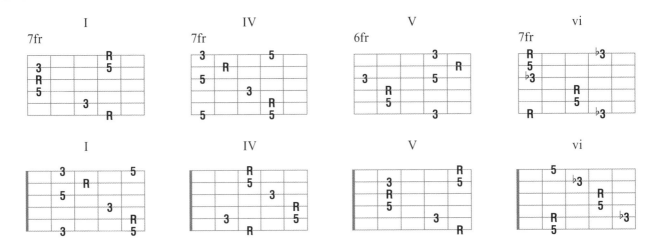

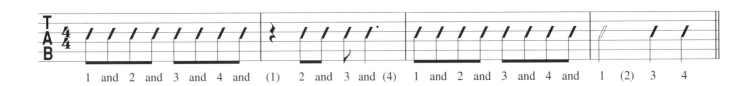

1 and 2 and 3 and 4 and   (1) 2 and 3 and (4)   1 and 2 and 3 and 4 and   1 (2) 3   4

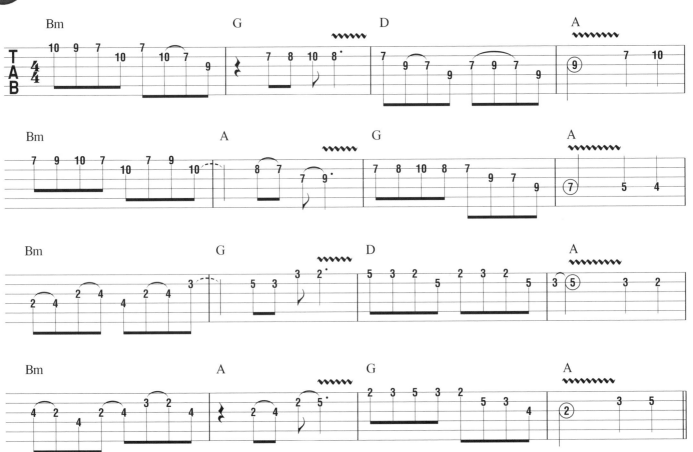

CHAPTER 11:

NEW PENTATONIC SCALE WITH POSITION SHIFT

Now that you've had a chance to absorb our new scale position, let's expand the scale by utilizing slides. Much like our previous fingering, we will begin by expanding the upper end of the scale. Study the scale diagrams shown below and notice that, in this pattern, the slide occurs on string 2. Using our alternate fingering (i.e., without the pinky) sets up the easiest way to execute the position shift.

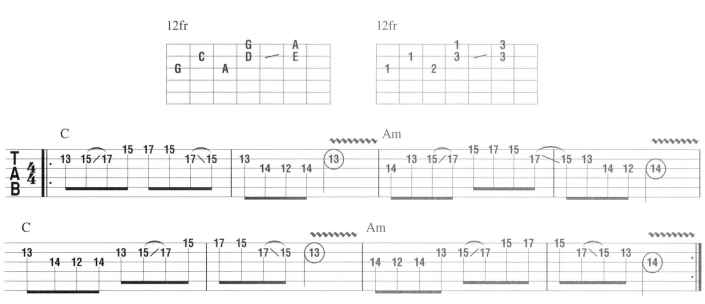

This next example illustrates a few ways to utilize the new pattern, including incorporating unison slides and a slide on string 1.

Continuing onward, we will move the same concept to the next octave, with the slide occurring on string 4.

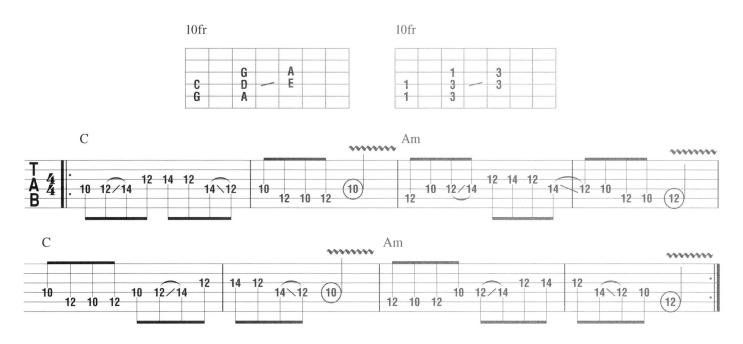

Try to play this familiar phrase in the new octave.

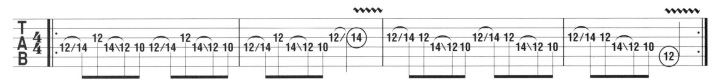

Our third slide in this position occurs on the 6th string and takes us into yet another octave.

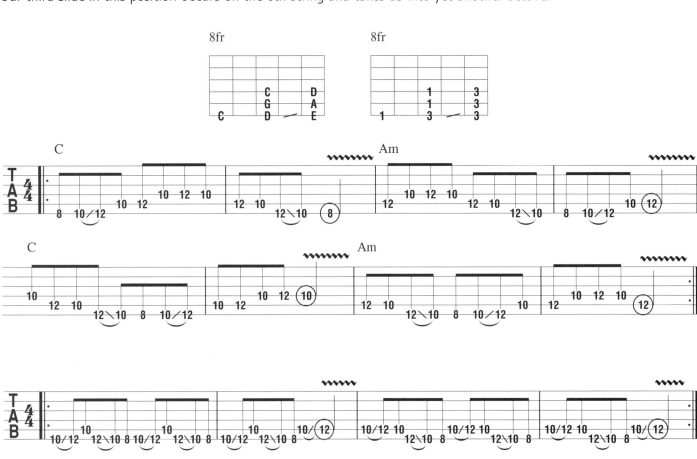

Now that we have played each octave of the scale individually, we are ready to combine them and look at the scale in its entirety. Before doing so, look at the three diagrams below and observe the symmetry of the patterns, which will aid greatly in visualizing the scale on the fretboard.

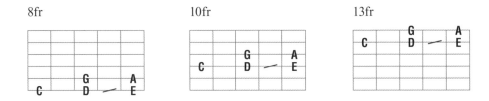

As you practice connecting all three patterns, observe the scale's highest and lowest points. The low C on fret 8 (string 6) connects the pattern to the first scale position that you learned; the high A on fret 17 (string 1) connects the pattern to the same fingering, an octave higher up the neck. Consequently, this fingering is incredibly useful for getting from one position to the next, as it is a three-fret shift away in either direction.

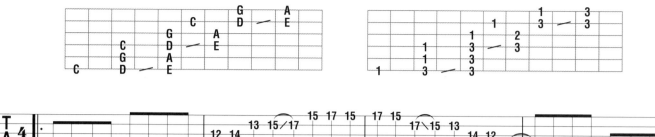

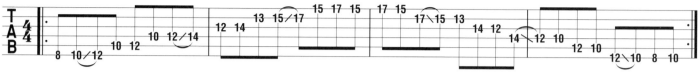

C–F–G–Am Solo

C Major / A Minor Pentatonic Scale

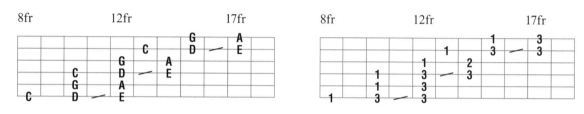

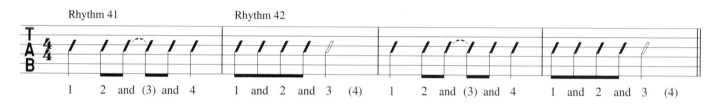

DEMO TRACK 46 BACKING TRACK 76

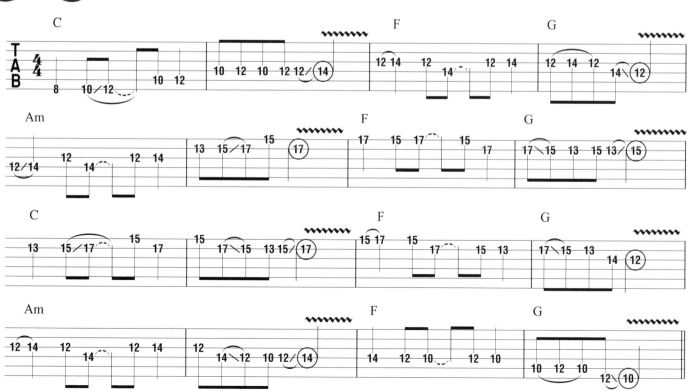

G Major / E Minor Pentatonic Scale

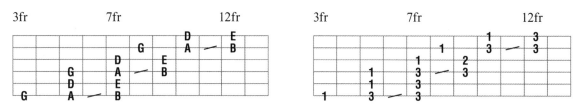

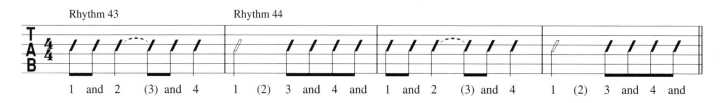

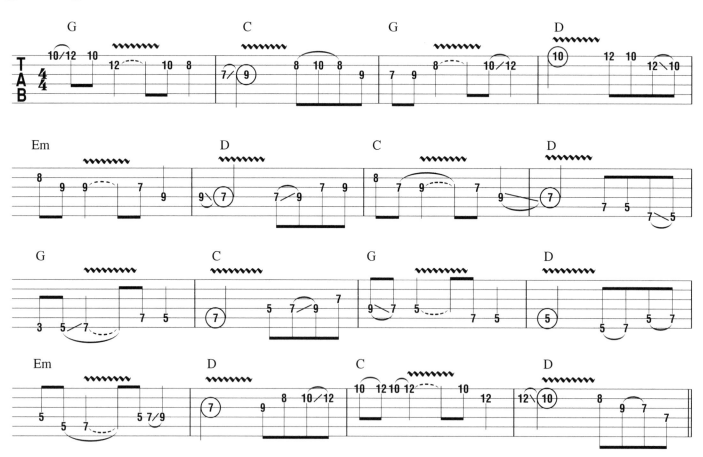

A–D–E–F#m Solo

A Major / F# Minor Pentatonic Scale

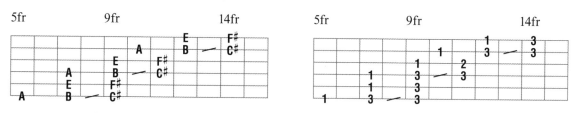

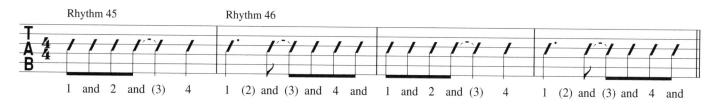

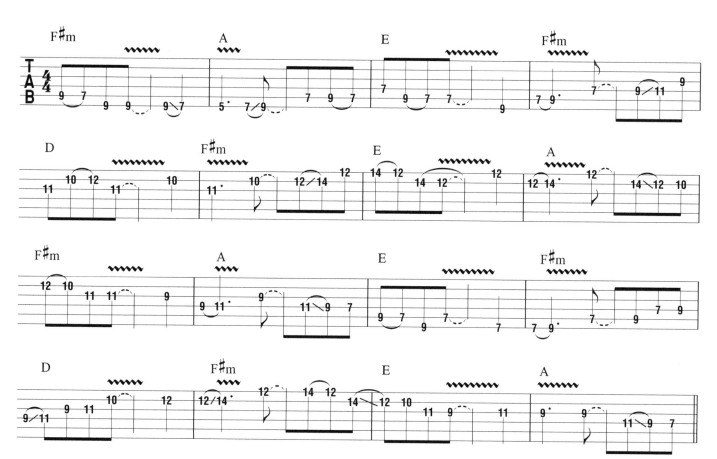

E Major / C# Minor Pentatonic Scale

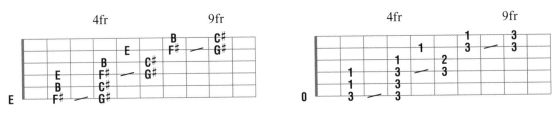

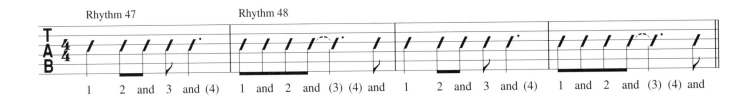

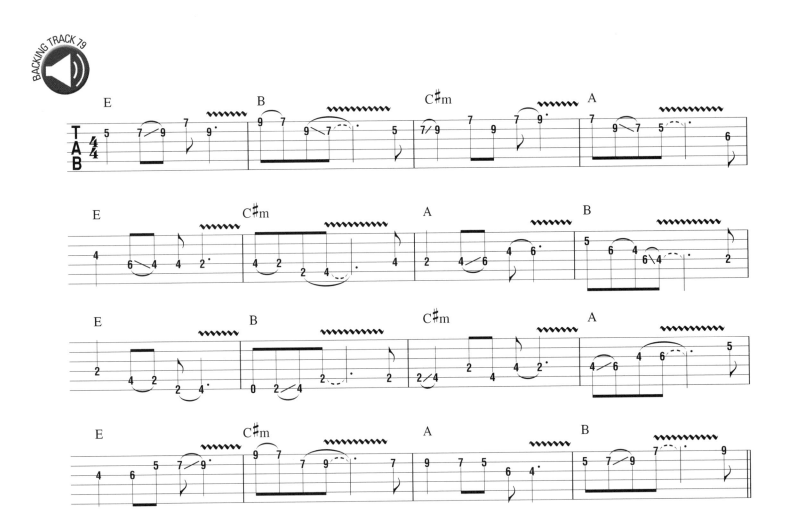

D–G–A–Bm Solo

D Major / B Minor Pentatonic Scale

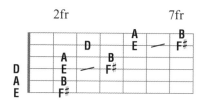 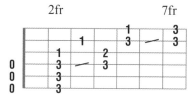

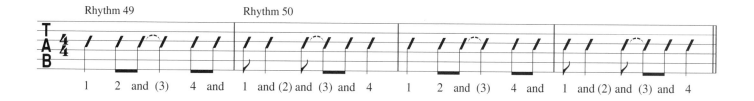

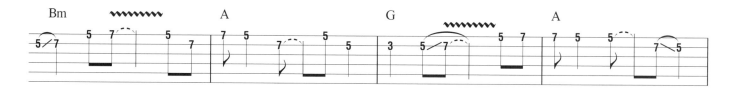

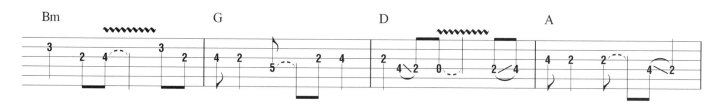

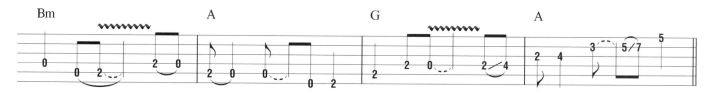

103

G–C–D–Em Solo (Rhythm Review)

G Major / E Minor Pentatonic Scale

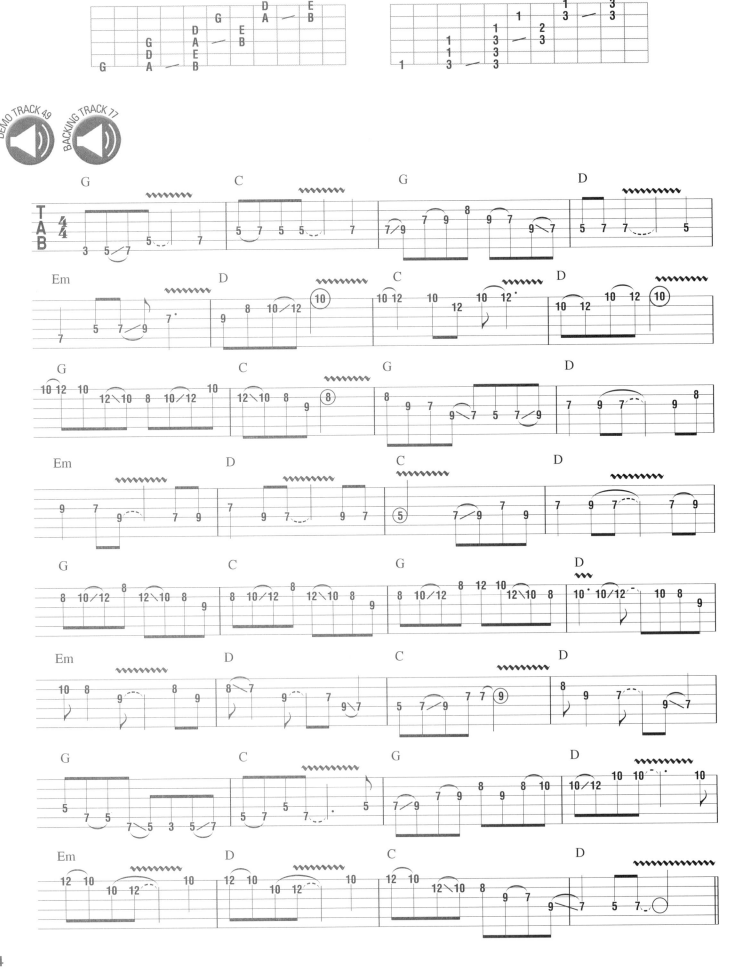

CHAPTER 12:

BENDING STRINGS

In addition to the techniques that you've learned so far, bending strings is one of the guitar's most unique traits, as well as one of the most expressive elements that you can add to your solos. While it is possible to bend nearly any note on the guitar, some notes traditionally lend themselves to bending more than others. Those notes most often are found on the top three strings, which, physically, are the easiest to bend. Also, those notes often are the highest note on a given string in the position in which you are playing. Examine the scale diagrams below. Each circled pitch commonly is bent up a whole step.

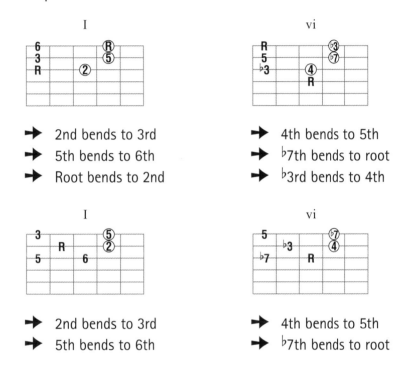

➡ 2nd bends to 3rd
➡ 5th bends to 6th
➡ Root bends to 2nd

➡ 4th bends to 5th
➡ ♭7th bends to root
➡ ♭3rd bends to 4th

➡ 2nd bends to 3rd
➡ 5th bends to 6th

➡ 4th bends to 5th
➡ ♭7th bends to root

To execute a bend, begin on the 3rd string, pushing it upwards, towards the ceiling. To facilitate the bend, you must reinforce the bend with another finger. Since placing additional fingers behind the finger that is fretting the note will not affect the note's pitch, place your middle finger behind your ring finger, as shown below. For support, let your thumb rest on top of the neck. Also, let your wrist move as you push the note up a whole step.

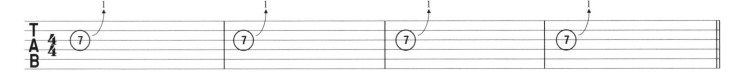

TIPS FOR STRING BENDING

➜ Use light-gauge strings until you build up strength;

➜ Always reinforce bends with an additional finger(s), as bending notes with one finger is extremely difficult. Adding another finger behind the note that you are bending gives you extra strength and, more importantly, more control of the pitch. If you bend with your pinky, try reinforcing it with your middle and ring fingers;

➜ Use the tips of your fingers, insuring that the note stays connected to the fret throughout the entire bend and/or release;

➜ Over-bending typically is worse than under-bending a note. You always can push a bend up a little more; however, once you are sharp, there is no going back;

➜ Take your time getting to your destination pitch. Slowly bending to pitch will help you remain aware of your tuning and prevent over-bending.

BENDING EXERCISES

Learning to bend strings while keeping the notes in tune can take much time and practice, but the sonic rewards that you receive are well worth the effort. Let's begin by concentrating on bending notes to pitch. Here, we will concentrate on matching a pitch to which you would typically slide (i.e., unison slides). As you play the following exercises, carefully listen to the fretted pitches, concentrating on matching them with the bent notes.

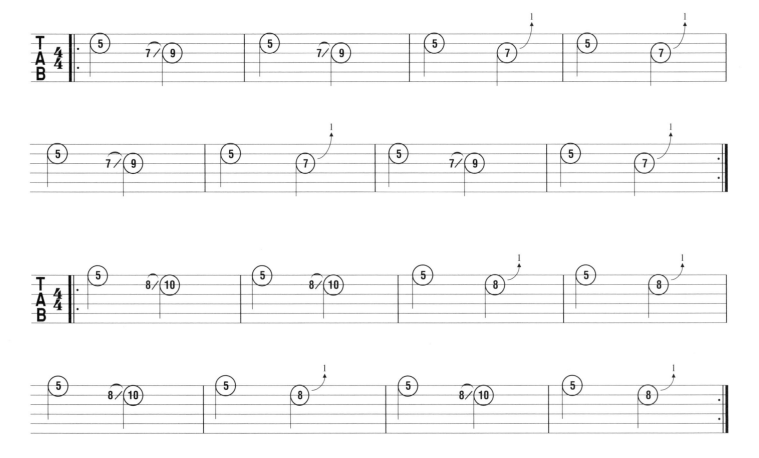

Sometimes, 1st-string bends can result in more tension than bends on strings 3 or 2. Since string 1 has no unison note to match, slide into the destination note before matching it with the bend.

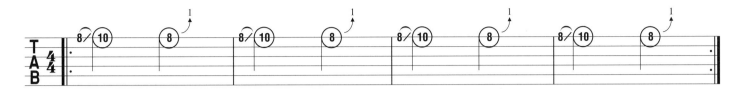

Now let's move these exercises up the neck, to our next position.

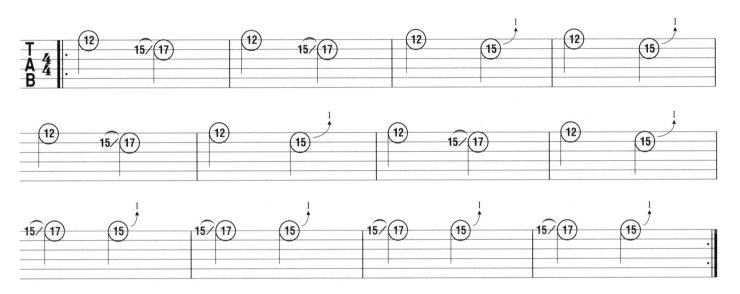

BENDING IN RHYTHM

Much like slides, hammer-ons, and pull-offs, bending can be used to articulate a note without picking the string again. To explore this idea, we will revisit some of the rhythms that we've used throughout the previous chapters. Pick the note with the fret number, as indicated, then use the bend to complete the rhythm.

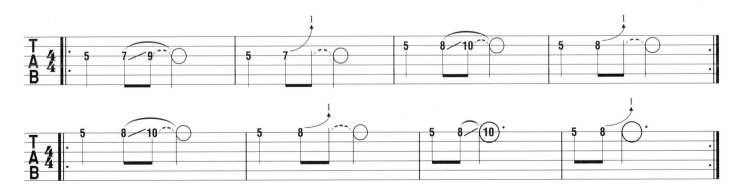

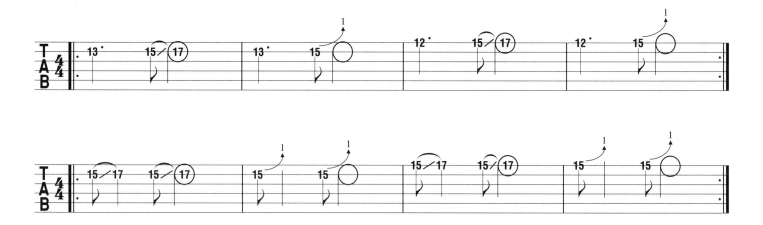

Like an upward bend, releasing a bend to its original pitch also can be used to sound a note without picking the string again. To accomplish this, the note must remain in contact with the fret throughout the course of the entire bend and release (up and down). Make sure that you are using your fingertips and that you pick only the first note. The "released" notes are shown in parentheses.

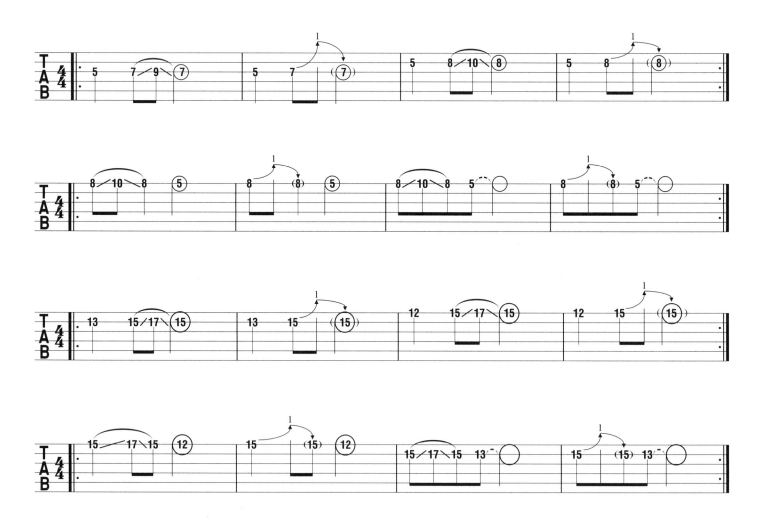

C–F–G–Am Solo

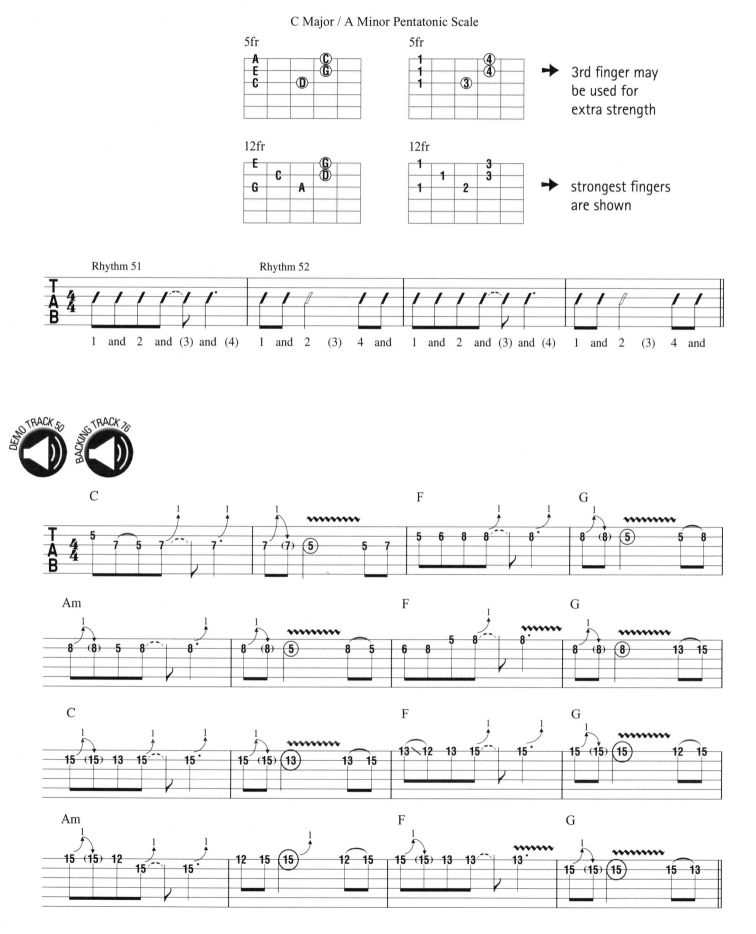

G Major / E Minor Pentatonic Scale

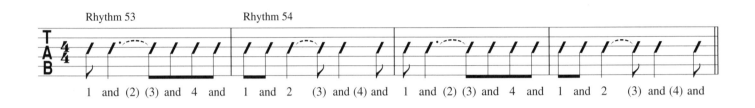

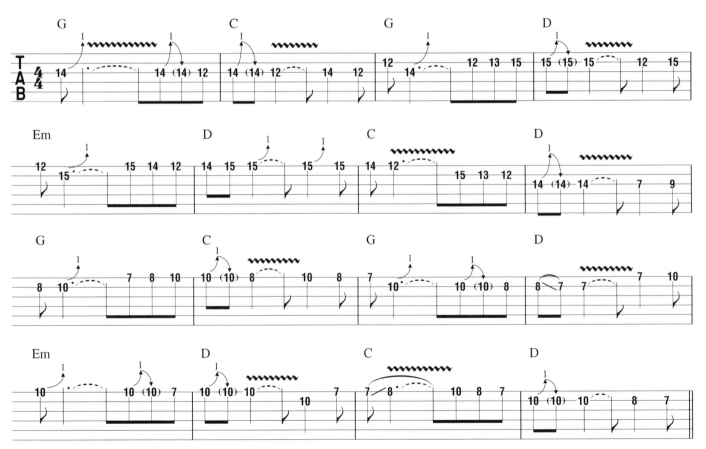

A Major / F# Minor Pentatonic Scale

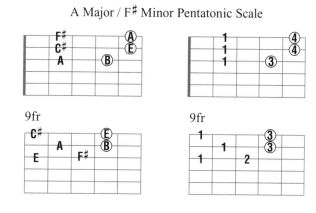

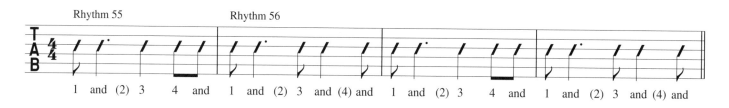

E Major / C# Minor Pentatonic Scale

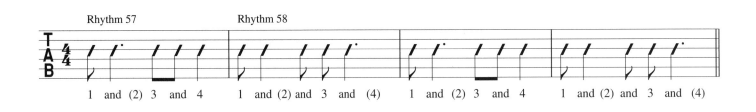

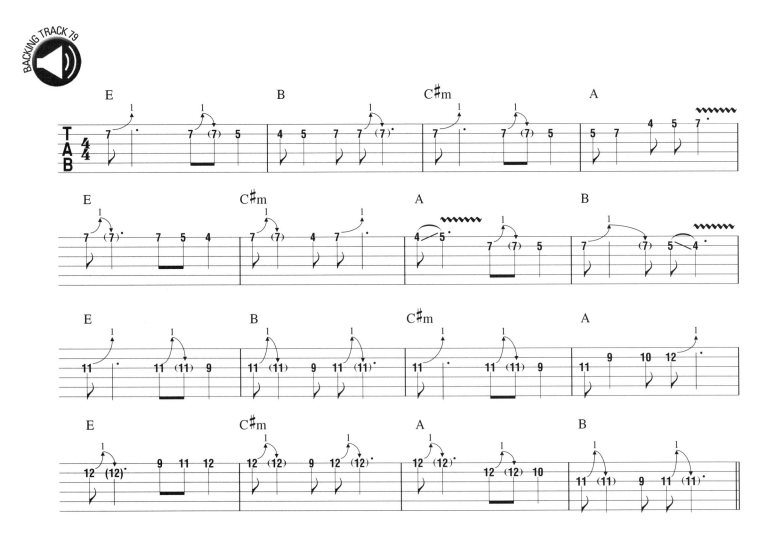

D Major / B Minor Pentatonic Scale

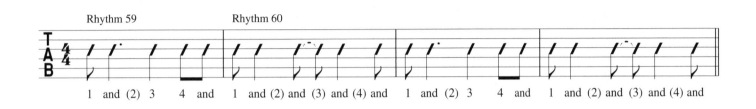

E–A–B–C♯m Solo (Rhythm Review)

E Major / C♯m Pentatonic Scale

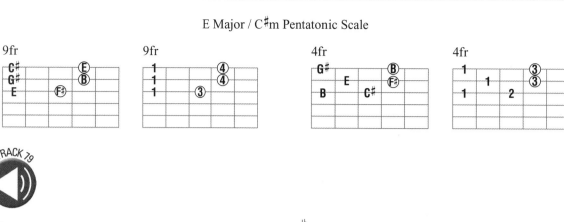

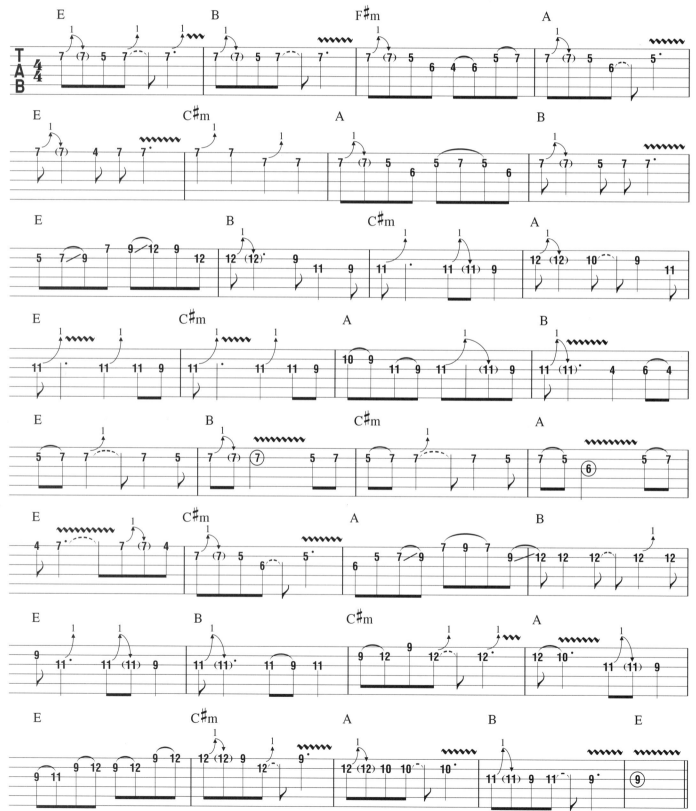

RHYTHM REVIEW

Before moving forward, let's review the 20 five-note rhythm patterns we've just learned. Count each pattern out loud before going back to the backing tracks and improvising with them. Feel free to mix and match them with the 3- and 4-note rhythms from the previous chapters.

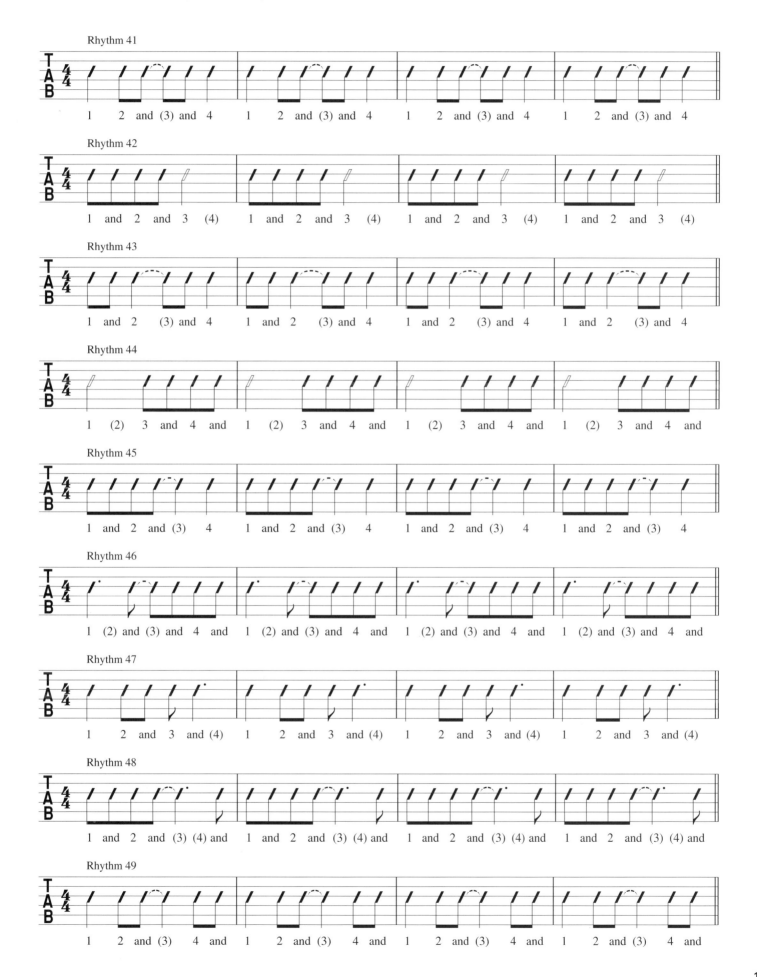

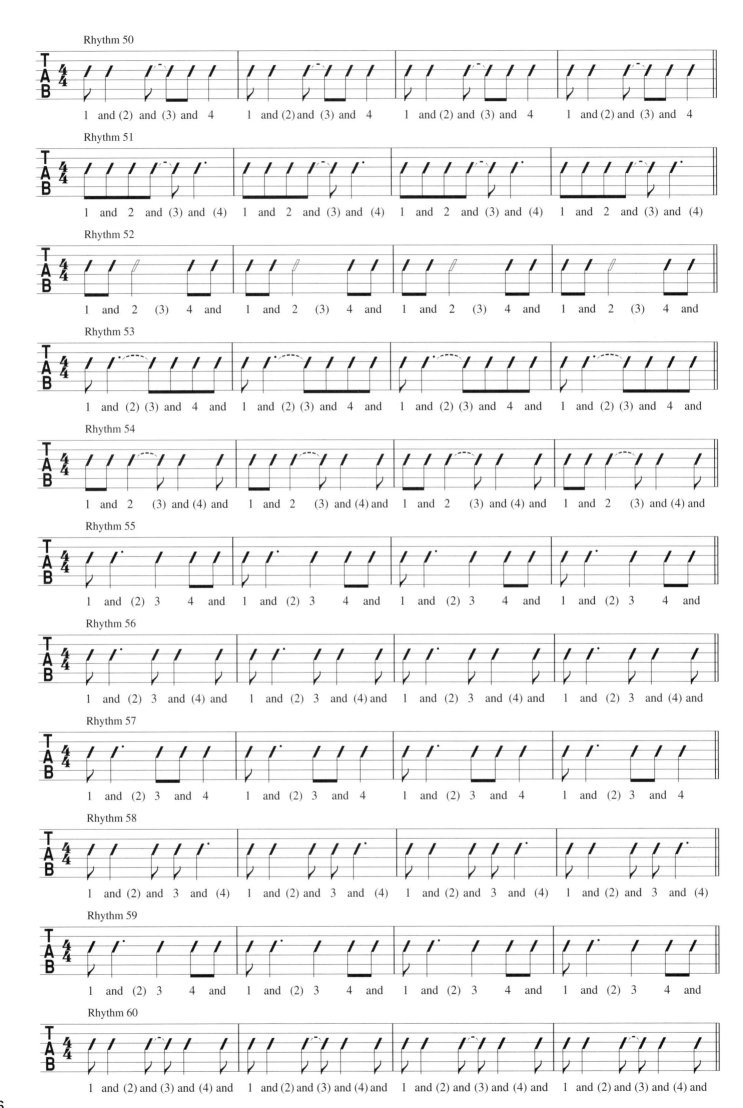

CHAPTER 13:

PUTTING IT ALL TOGETHER

If you have made it to this point in the book—congratulations!—you have absorbed quite a bit of information and amassed a large vocabulary of concepts from which to draw. Now the time has come to put it all to use, and the final five solos will do just that. Before learning them, let's take stock of all the musical devices that we've incorporated so far.

Finding the Strongest Notes: The notes that are part of the chord that you are playing over will always be the most consonant notes on which to end your phrases. Use your ears and intuition to tell you whether a note is creating tension or release. When in the practice room, using your head to think about what notes are in the chord is a great way to draw associations with how the notes sound and resolve. However, in the heat of the moment, the goal is to let the music flow. Too much thinking can interrupt the process; using your ears perhaps is the most important concept of this book.

Rhythm and Phrasing: Equally as important as what note you are playing is *when* and *where* you place them. By this point, we have utilized 60 different rhythms and combined three-, four-, and five-note phrases. By doing so, the groundwork has been laid for you to create your own rhythms and to venture into six- and seven-note phrases. After all, rhythm combinations are infinite.

Additionally, incorporating the melodic patterns that you've learned enables you to string rhythmic ideas together or to build momentum between ideas. Be sure to reference the rhythm reviews and the melodic pattern pages to assist you with the construction of your own combinations, then use them to improvise over the backing tracks of your choice.

Song Form: In this book, we have discussed three possible forms: AABA, ABAB, and ABAC. Each of them are useful for creating solos that evolve and tell a story. Again, feel free to create your own forms. A few examples are: AAAB, AABC, or ABBA. You even can elongate the forms by making each section two-plus measures long. The only limit is your imagination!

Scales and Fingerings: Through examination of countless guitar solos in various musical styles, it is apparent that the most common melodic concept is to alternate phrasing between the pentatonic scale and the major scale. Generally, the pentatonic scale is a popular choice due to its sound and the fact that only two notes cause tension, the 2nd and the 6th. Mixing in the major scale gives us two more tension notes (the 4th and the 7th) and enables the use of more chord tones when on a chord other than the I. Utilizing the two main scale areas that we have examined will provide you with the tools to play in several octaves, with many articulation possibilities. Explore different ways to get from one position to the next.

Vibrato: If you're letting it ring, make it sing! A smooth and vocal-like vibrato, rather than an out-of-tune quiver, is the mark of a seasoned guitarist and a guaranteed way to make your solos emotionally effective.

Articulation: In addition to the aforementioned devices, the way you articulate the phrases that you create can give interesting variations to a musical idea. Bending and sliding are a great way to add a vocal-like quality to a phrase. Hammer-ons and pull-offs not only will affect the sound of the notes, but also make difficult phrases easier to play.

As you practice the next five example solos, keep an eye out for all of the aforementioned musical devices, noting how many of them you can identify. After playing the solos, go back and freely improvise over the backing tracks on the CD. You will discover that the ideas you've practiced throughout this book will flow out naturally, just like a conversation. After all, music is a language. Speak it often!

C–F–G–Am Solo

C Major / A Minor Scale Patterns

G–C–D–Em Solo

G Major / E Minor Scale Patterns

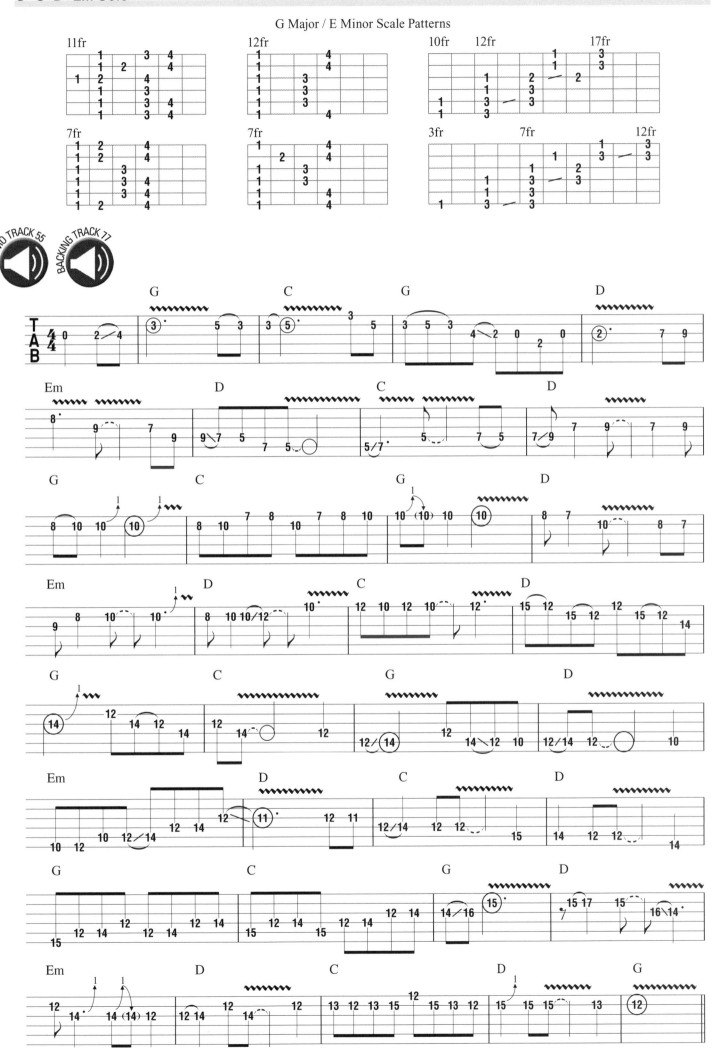

A Major / F# Minor Scale Patterns

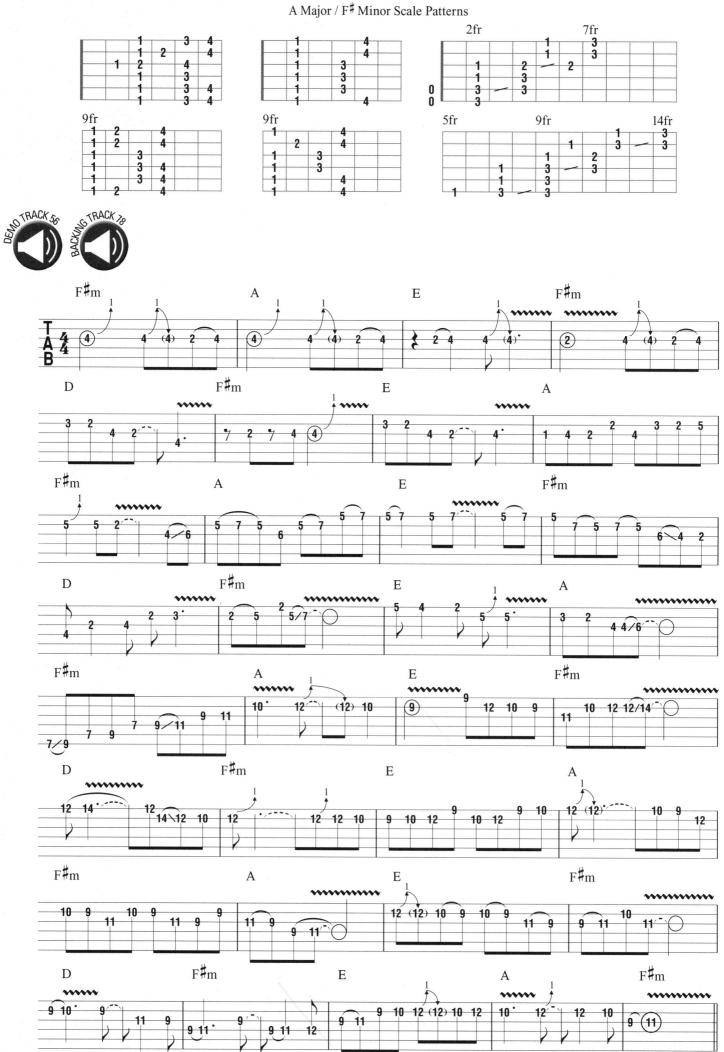

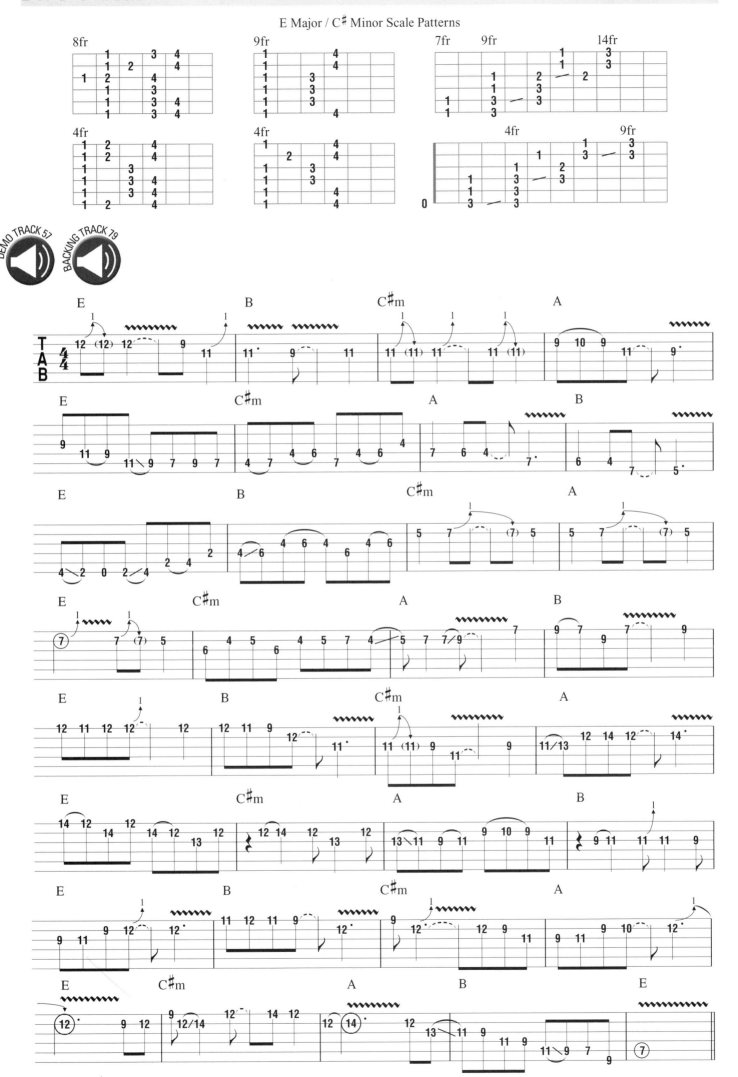

D Major / B Minor Scale Patterns

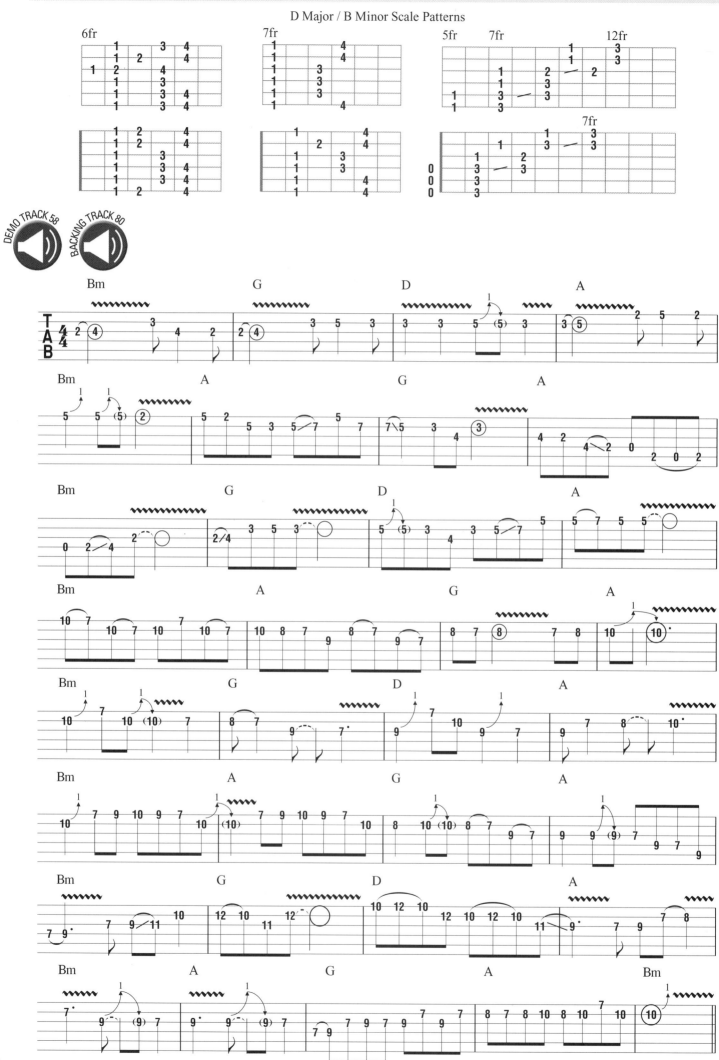

BACKING TRACKS

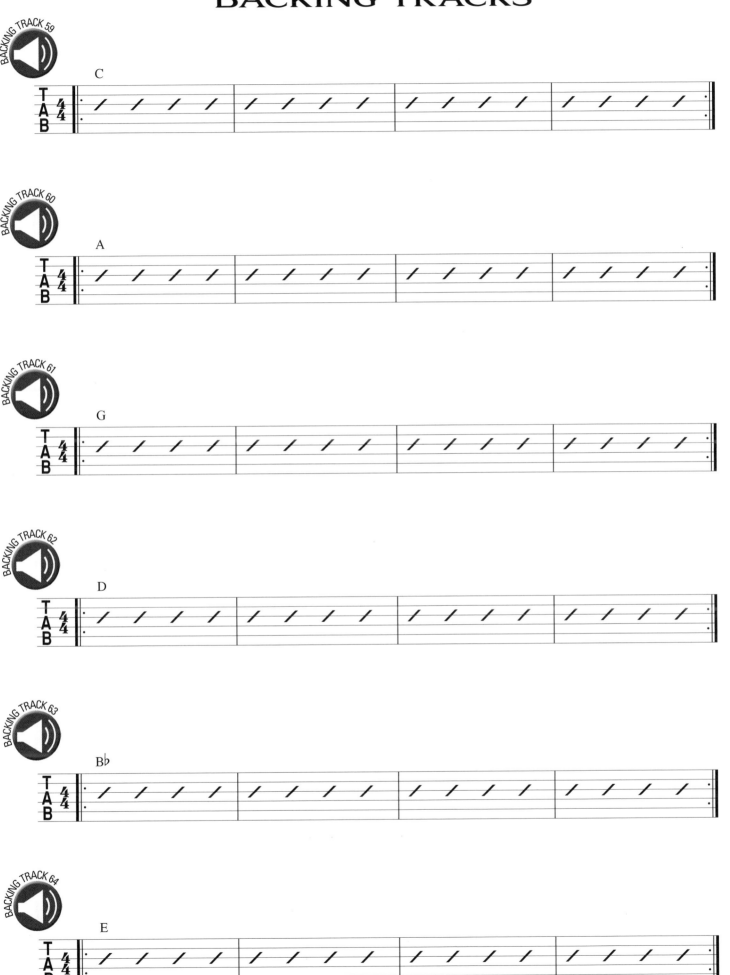

BACKING TRACK 65

Eb

BACKING TRACK 66

Am

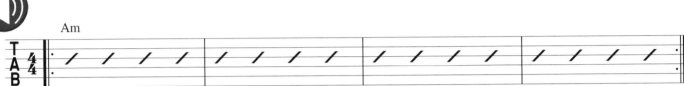

BACKING TRACK 67

Cm

BACKING TRACK 68

Em

BACKING TRACK 69

Gm

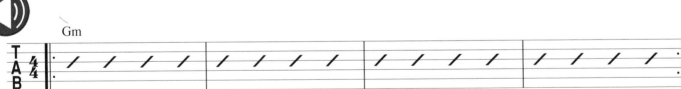

BACKING TRACK 70

Dm

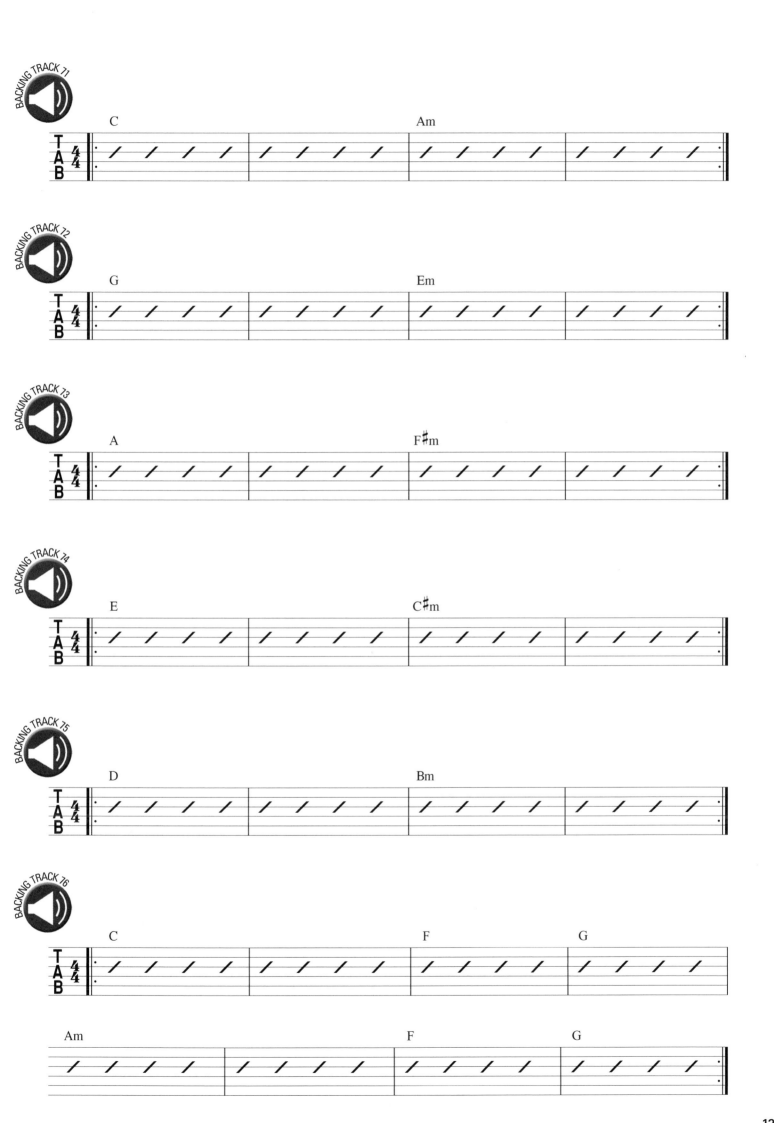

G	C	G	D

Em	D	C	D

F#m	A	E	F#m

D	F#m	E	A

E	B	C#m	A

E	C#m	A	B

Bm	G	D	A

Bm	A	G	A